Listening
to Families
REFRAMING SERVICES

Mehrunnisa Ali

Patricia Corson

Elaine Frankel

Published by Chestnut Publishing Group
4005 Bayview Avenue, Suite 610
Toronto, ON M2M 3Z9 Canada
Tel: 416 224-5824   Fax: 416 224-0595
www. chestnutpublishing.com

Typesetting & Design: Laura Brady

National Library of Canada Cataloguing in Publication
Ali, Mehrunnisa Ahmad
Listening to families : reframing services / Mehrunnisa Ahmad Ali, Patricia Corson, Elaine Frankel.

Includes bibliographical references.
ISBN 978-1-894601-45-0

1. Family—Services for—Canada. 2. Family—Canada.
I. Corson, Patricia, 1949– II. Frankel, Elaine B., 1945– III. Title.

HV700.C3A45 2009   362.82'80971   C2009-903394-1

We acknowledge the financial support of the government of Canada through the Book Publishing Industry Development Program (BPIDP) for our publishing activities.

CONTENTS

Acknowledgments

We owe gratitude to many people for this work. Our research assistants Farishta Dinshaw, Bhavani Ranganathan, Charity-Anne Hannan, Olga Fellus, and above all Amanda Ajodhia-Andrews, contributed to this work at various times with enthusiasm, patience, and good humour. The Ontario Leaders' willingness to experiment with the idea, their participation in the simulation exercise while being video-taped, and their generosity in sharing their experience of developing the narratives were invaluable. For this we would like to thank: Tony Travo, Barb Brown, Paula Hathaway, Wendy Wilson, Rosetta Racco, and Astrid Soto. The Canadian Leaders Tracey Bink, Cassy Lawson, Anima Anand, Michele Hucul, Denise Currie, Wendy Wilson, Mariam Esmail, Mira Borejszo, Jackie Collins, Nicole Parsons, Darlene Lawrence, and Brenda Clarke took time away from their busy schedules to try out the narrative approach and to write to us about how it worked out. We are grateful for their faith in the idea, and their commitment to completing it in a timely fashion. Our Advisory Committee, consisting of Dr. Brenda Smith-Chant, Mario Calla, Natalie Chapman, Martha Lee-Blickstead, Janice Macaulay, Elizabeth Moffat, Daisy Talob, Lorraine Telford, and Jill Worthy met several times during the project to review our plans and products, and. most importantly, to talk about the narrative approach for the DVD. We learned much from their wisdom and their perspectives on how professionals in different fields might use this approach. We are particularly grateful to Janice Macaulay who carefully edited the manuscript which is now in your hands. Peter Mak of Makcom Media, who produced the DVD with remarkable patience and professionalism, and Harry Goldhar of Chestnut Publishing who edited and published the book with incredible dedication, guided us throughout the project. Our dear friend and former colleague Kenise Murphy Kilbride spent numerous voluntary hours editing our work to turn it into a coherent piece of work. We are very grateful for her generous spirit. We could not have managed to do this work without our Project Manager, Catherine Moher, whose ability to manage multiple tasks at short notice with good cheer is much appreciated. Although we cannot name them, we owe our deepest gratitude to the families who participated in this work. We and our colleagues in this project learned a lot from them, and we hope our students will continue to learn from their narratives.

This project is funded by the Government of Canada's Social Development Partnerships Program. The opinions and interpretations in this publication are those of the authors and do not necessarily reflect those of the Government of Canada.

Introduction

The *Listening to Families: Reframing Services* project is a response to the deep divide that can exist between Canadian public service institutions and contemporary families, particularly those who are marginalized in our society. Our individual concerns about such families intersected in this effort to reframe public services to work with and for such families. Mehrunnisa Ali's work focuses on newcomer children, youth, and families; Patricia Corson studies child development and the effects of poverty on children and families; and Elaine Frankel advocates for the inclusion of young children with disabilities and their families. This project is premised on our belief that if service providers, such as those who work in child care centres, schools, family support programs, early intervention services, health services, and social agencies, knew the rich and complex stories of the families they serve, they could develop more trusting and mutually supportive relationships with them. They could reach out to more families who are not benefiting from their services, and increase the usefulness of their work for families they already serve. Thus the purpose of this book and the accompanying DVD is to increase the capacity of providers of public services to engage with and respond to families who may not be well understood because they are newcomers to Canada, live in poverty, or have a child with a disability.

For this project we used the term 'newcomer' to refer to immigrants, refugees, refugee claimants and families without legal status who had arrived in Canada within the last five years. Not all members of these families necessarily speak English or French, they are relatively unfamiliar with Canadian institutions, and have fairly limited social networks. Defining families who live in poverty was more difficult. We thought asking families about their incomes would be intrusive, and even if we did have that information it would be difficult to assess if the family lived in poverty or not. We therefore relied on self-identification as a measure for including such families in this project. We defined disability as a broad category inclusive of physical, intellectual, or emotional exceptionalities, ranging from attention-deficit disorders to autism, and deafness to Down syndrome. Children with disabilities often need additional or different supports from their families as well as from service providers such as teachers, health care professionals, or social workers.

Our advocacy for people working in public services to learn more about and thus be more responsive to such families is based on three key assumptions. First, children's ability to benefit from public services is crucially dependent on their families' values, priorities, resources, and strategies for seeking and using support systems. Service providers in child care, health, education, recreation, and other social services therefore need to take into account these families' particular features in order to provide services that will meet their children's needs. Second, we believe that all children have the same rights to public services. The fact that some of them are disadvantaged because of their families' particular circumstances should not mean that they have to relinquish their right to benefit from public services offered by the state. Third, those who work in public services have the responsibility to figure out ways to interrupt the cycle of disadvantage that affects multiple generations in the same family. This responsibility is based on what Nel Noddings (2002, 2005) calls "the ethic of care". Noddings tells us that ethical caring is the sense of moral obligation associated with our professional role. It requires the creation and nurturing of caring relationships, and a commitment to thinking with and on behalf of others, through attentive listening and dialogue. She suggests that a society composed of people who habitually draw on a well-established ideal of caring will move towards social policies that are consonant with principles of justice and equity (2002). Other scholars (*e.g.*, Gilligan, 1995, Nussbaum, 1996) affirm that when structures of public institutions are shaped by ethical caring, they help us move collectively from self-interest to conduct that is more just and equitable.

The structures of public service institutions in Canada are based for the most part on the world views, assumptions, and lifestyles of British and French settlers and their descendents. The policies and practices in these institutions are limited by the boundaries of their knowledge and experience. However, Canada's population is becoming rapidly more diverse in terms of cultural beliefs and practices, socio-economic status, and physical or intellectual ability. Immigration alone is adding about 250,000 people to our population every year and according to the census data for 2006, about 22% of Canada's population was born outside this country (Statistics Canada, 2008). Nearly one fifth of the annual new arrivals (50,000) are made up of children below the age of 15 years. Canadian institutions are legally and ethically committed to providing services such as schooling, child care, healthcare, and sometimes child protection to these children. What do service providers need to know to reach these children with timely and appropriate services?

Canada's population is also growing more diverse in terms of income levels as the middle class is shrinking and differences between the income levels of the rich and the poor are increasing markedly (Statistics Canada, 2008). According to a recent report, nearly 760,000 of Canada's children live in poverty (Campaign 2000, 2008). What do service providers, who usually belong to the middle class, need to know about how poverty affects the lives of children and their families?

Children with a variety of disabilities are also becoming a more visible part of our population as we begin to acknowledge their human rights to lead fulfilling lives and our obligations as a society to make that possible. Although accurate figures are not currently available, an estimated 5-7% of children and youth have disabilities ranging from visual impairment to autism (Canadian Association for Community Living, 2008). What do we need to know to meet our obligations to these children and their families?

These features of families often overlap, compounding their impact on young children. For example, in Canada child poverty is prevalent among 49% of newcomers who arrived between 1996 and 2001, 34% among 'visible' minorities and 27.7% among children with disabilities (Campaign 2000, 2007). Families who are dealing with multiple disadvantages find it additionally difficult to represent and advocate for themselves. The institutional structures of public services do not create opportunities for such families to be listened to.

Services for young children and their families are conceptualized, organized, and offered in ways that do not take into account the realities of families who are different from the 'mainstream' population. This is primarily because individuals or groups who typically provide the services, and/or make decisions about how they should be provided, may have very little information about families who are different from their own. Newcomers to Canada, families living in poverty, and those who have a child with a disability are not always included in these decisions. In the absence of sufficient and accurate information, service providers may assume that families they are working with are similar to their own, or reflect the stereotypes they have constructed on the basis of prior personal experiences, codified knowledge in popular literature, or media representations.

To address this issue, we began with a pilot project funded by the Faculty of Community Services in Ryerson University. This project enabled us to develop and test our approach to collecting 'narratives' of three families, each representing one of the three kinds of marginality mentioned above. Subsequently, a three-year national project was funded by the Department of Human Resources and Skills Development, Government of Canada, Social Development Partnerships Program, to conduct the study on a larger scale and produce this book and the accompanying DVD.

In the first phase of the project two staff members from each of three Ontario-based family support programs (also known as Family Resource Programs, Early Years Centres, Community Development Programs, and by other similar names) were asked to replicate the work we had done in the pilot project. We called these researchers the Ontario Leaders and trained them in using the narrative approach through an intensive two-day workshop, using professional actors to simulate the experiences of families we had interviewed in the pilot project. This allowed us to fine-tune the interview guide (See Appendix II) we had developed, and the Ontario Leaders to sharpen their interviewing skills. The Ontario Leaders then recruited families from their own areas of service, representing the three designated categories of disadvantage, to participate in the project. Subsequently, they interviewed one or both adults in each family over three or four sessions, each lasting about an hour or so, about their histories, socio-economic activities, hopes and expectations for their children, strategies and resources they used for meeting their goals, challenges they faced, and the nature and forms of support they would like from public services. These interviews were audio-taped, fully transcribed, and then recursively edited by the interviewers, the family, and the research team into family narratives.

The Ontario Leaders then invited colleagues from other institutional services in their neighbourhood, such as child care, schools, public health, and social welfare to a workshop where they presented their work and facilitated a discussion on whether it was desirable and possible for them to develop and use family narratives in their work. Using their own experiences, as well as the feedback they received at the workshops, the Ontario Leaders then helped us train staff from six other family support programs from across Canada to use the narrative approach with families in their own geographic regions. Meanwhile, the three of us organized videotaped interviews with members of our Advisory Committee, who served in senior professional positions in education, public health, child care, family support programs, and social work, to comment on the potential value and barriers to developing family narratives in the institutional contexts of various public services. (All of the narratives - three from the pilot project, nine from the Ontario region, and eighteen from across Canada - are included as Appendix I).

This book and accompanying DVD are designed, first, to make a case for why it is so important for service providers to listen to families, not just through brief conversations in corridors, but systematically and with full attention, to effectively work with them and their children. We suggest that they learn as much as they can about families they serve, particularly those who are different from their own, in order to meet the ethical standards of their professional practice.

This book and the accompanying DVD are also designed to help service providers:

a) consider the family narratives included here for designing or adapting their own services or programs,
b) use the package for in-service and pre-service training for those who work or will work in public service institutions,
c) develop similar narratives based on other families in their own professional contexts. [See DVD: Introduction.]

The next chapter discusses the broad concept of the family as a social institution. It includes a discussion on functions of parent-child relations, the impact of changing social contexts on families, and the reasons why public services do not easily adapt to diverse families. Chapter Three provides an overview of the three kinds of circumstances that lead to the marginalization of families: newcomer status, poverty, and having a child with a disability. Chapter Four introduces the reader to the use of narrative as a meaning-making process in professional fields. The transformative nature of telling and listening to family narratives is explored from the perspectives of families, the individual service providers, and the institution where they work. With the background now in place, Chapter Five provides a step-by-step guide to the process of developing family narratives. Strategies for effective listening and details on how to conduct the interview, transcribe, and write up the narrative are explained. Chapter Six focuses on the use of family narratives for reframing services through in-service and pre-service education.

The family narratives are included in this book as examples for those who wish to develop narratives of families in their own professional contexts, or as resource materials for those who want to use them for instructional purposes in professional development or pre-service training. A comprehensive bibliography and web site links are also provided.

We sincerely hope you will consider using the narrative approach in your work as service providers, or as educators of current and future service providers. Colleagues who have used it tell us that it has transformed the way they view families, and the way they work with families.

The Child and the Family

The family into which a child is born places the child in a culture, a community, a society, and a time in history. All these contexts influence the interactions within the family and the way the family interacts has a very powerful effect on the psychosocial development of the child. (Martin & Corson, 2007, p. 111)

The dependency relationship between the child and her family in the human species has remained remarkably resistant to change. Whether a child is born into a high- or a low-income family, a remote rural location or a crowded mega-city, or a male- or female-only household, she remains crucially dependent on her family for a very long time. Everywhere in the world, a child's family is responsible for ensuring her physical, emotional, intellectual, and social health and well being. In economically well-developed countries, publicly funded social institutions such as child care centres, schools, public health centres, and social welfare agencies have been set up to support families in meeting their children's needs. While the availability, accessibility, and affordability of these services vary a great deal across and within nation-states, a child's ability to benefit from them is always mediated by her family. In countries that are less economically developed, systems of interdependence among generations, relatives, friends, and neighbours have evolved for meeting the needs of the young. The kind of care a child receives in such contexts is also mediated by her family's values, resources, and networks.

Many family concepts

While all of us have been members of at least one family, and may have some personal definitions of what a family is, there is little consensus in different societies about what the term means. In some parts of the world everyone who lives in the same dwelling, including children, their parents, grandparents, aunts and uncles, and sometimes their spouses and children as well, are considered one family. In others, this unit would be called an extended family, while only a nuclear family, *i.e.*, children and their parents, would be considered a family.

In Canada, the term family continues to be defined in different ways for different purposes. The census defines a family as a married couple, with or without never-married children of either spouse, a common-law couple with or without children, or a lone parent with never-married children living in the same dwelling (Statistics Canada, 2008). Recent changes in the law have enabled gay couples to be explicitly included in definitions of families. Immigration authorities consider parents of the adult who sponsors migration to be members of his or her family. Both adopted and foster children cared for by one or more adults are considered members of a family by institutions such as schools and health clinics, but only adopted children have the legal right to financial support by their parents.

The concept of family has become further complicated in the last few decades as a result of advances in medical sciences. Children born from cells contributed by a male and a female, prenatally grown in the body of another female, are biologically connected to all those adults but may not be members of their families. Legal and ethical issues arising from such arrangements are common. Nevertheless, for most practical purposes, children who live together in a household, but may or may not be biologically related, and adults who take care of them, are considered a family. Adults who have the legal and primary responsibility for caring for the children play the role of parents. Social institutions hold them responsible for the well-being of the children until they reach adulthood, or the legal age of majority.

Multiple and changing roles of families

Parents and children in any family, irrespective of their social or geographic location, relate to each other in some predictable ways. The main functions of the parents in the family are to protect, nurture, and socialize the young. They may be helped in performing these functions by older children in the family, relatives, or paid employees, but they are the ones ultimately responsible for ensuring that their children's needs are met.

Heath (2006) lists six functions of the parenting role, and claims that parents draw upon general empirical and theoretical knowledge, as well as specific knowledge about the child's characteristics, to fulfill these roles.

Further, Heath asserts that "Parents work best when they know what to expect in general and in relation to a specific child" (p.758). Citing Holden and Hawk (2003) she claims that parental behaviours are guided by their "social cognition" (inter-related processes of anticipating, assessing, problem-solving and reflecting) and meta-cognition in relation to parenting.

Parenting functions obviously change as a result of the growth and development of the child and changes within the family, as well as changes in the family's external circumstances. Typically, as a child grows, she becomes more independent in meeting her physical needs within the familiar environment of the home. However, she still needs adult protection outside the home for much longer. Parenting functions may also change as a result of changes within the family, such as the birth of another child, changes in the adults' partnerships, illness or death. A parent may need to teach the child how to interact with a new sibling or the new adult in the family, or learn how to manage without a parent if one is no longer available. Changes in external circumstances are also difficult for the family as the adults as well as the children learn to deal with them at the same time.

Care

One special function of parenting is that of caring, and it deserves special attention here. The word 'care' comprises a variety of meanings. Noddings (2003), for example, defines care as "a state of mental suffering or of engrossment: to care is to be in a burdened mental state, one of anxiety, fear, or solicitude about something or someone" (p. 9). Care may also mean that an individual has a particular "regard for or inclination toward that something or someone" (p. 9). It may also indicate a kind of safekeeping of someone or something (p. 9). Furthermore, Noddings considers the concept of caring as a reflective process that requires one to perceive situations, needs, and expectations from the other's viewpoint.

Freeman describes four stages of caring: "1) experiencing caring, 2) practising caring, 3) initiating and sustaining caring relationships, and 4) continuing caring reflections and refinements" (as cited in Nowak-Fabrykowski & Caldwell, 2002, p. 358-359). Helping individuals progress, evolve, and gain a greater understanding of themselves are functions of caring (Nowak-Fabrykowski & Caldwell, 2002). Noddings (2003) indicates that the "one caring" actively engages and listens to the "cared-for", often receptively taking on the emotions which the cared-for shares (p. 19). At the same time, the cared-for experiences a sense of growth, feeling that "something has been added to him [or her]" (p. 20). Similarly, Mayeroff stipulates that the act of caring supports the individual's 'growth' in which he or she may achieve a greater awareness of the self (as cited in Noddings, 2002, p. 12). It is clear that through caring, a relationship develops between the cared-for and the one caring (Noddings, 2003), one of "shared control" (Noddings, 2002, p. 14). However, Noddings maintains that the relationship fostered through caring is not founded in pity, but rather it is one of empathy rooted within affirmative interpersonal relationships (as cited in Shields, 2004). We may note as an aside that service providers working with families often view themselves as care providers.

Marginalized families

Bronfenbrenner's ecological model (1979, 1986) is a useful framework for understanding how familial processes influence, and are influenced by external conditions and changes in those conditions. This model identifies the nested locations of individuals within families, within communities and within the larger social milieu. It also emphasizes the multi-directional influences of these contexts in shaping children's developmental trajectories. Each of these contextual spheres influences the others, and also mediates the effects of the others. Parents, for example, mediate the influence of the school or neighbourhood on the child, and also mediate on behalf of the child in the school or neighbourhood.

In general, larger systems exert greater influence on smaller ones, and are less permeable to change. For example, statutory school attendance in Canada requires that parents send their children to school at a certain age for a specific duration in the day. School hours do not match most parents' working hours. Parents have to make alternative arrangements for their children's after-school supervision but have not managed to change school hours. Changes in large systems take a long time because they involve many people, financial resources, and rules and regulations that have become a part of decision-makers' assumptions about how things should work.

However, change can begin in smaller systems and gradually spread to larger ones. In Canada, parents who do not want to send their children to local public schools have the right to educate them at home, as long as they subject their home-schooling to periodic inspections by public school authorities. Some of these parents, along with other members of their communities, have managed to set up privately funded schools, usually religiously based, where they teach languages, values, religious and social practices that are not taught in public schools to young members of their community.

Changing or modifying a larger system to meet their children's needs is particularly difficult for individual families or even groups of families who have less political power than members of the dominant mainstream society (Gordon & Nocon, 2008; Harris & Goodall, 2008; Turney & Kao, 2009). Members of established decision-making bodies tend to choose people from their own social circles, who are like themselves, to replace those who leave. People who are racially, ethnically, culturally, economically, or politically different from members of these groups are simply not invited to join these bodies. In the rare instances where they are included, they are perceived exclusively as representatives of minority groups with whom they are associated, and incapable of understanding issues that affect the majority. This severely curtails their ability to influence decisions that have wider, more significant implications.

Another reason why minority voices are not taken into consideration in institutional decision-making is that people who make those decisions may know very little about those who are different from them. This information gap is, firstly, due to the lack of informal social interactions among groups associated with different socio-economic classes, race or ethnicity, or physical or developmental ability. Economic status is a key determinant of housing and neighbourhoods. Families with high income levels socially interact with neighbouring families who have similar levels of income. Similarly, those who cannot afford expensive housing congregate in the low-income neighbourhoods. Racialized and ethnicized groups also tend to stay together as they feel a higher level of acceptance from people who look and behave like themselves. People with disabilities often lead very isolated lives because able people avoid any kind of social interaction with them. This makes it impossible for them to develop social bonds with people who are different from them.

Institutional mechanisms for collecting information about children and families are very limited in scope. When a child is admitted in a daycare centre or a school, everything that is considered significant about her and her family by the institution is expected to fit into a short form, with boxes to tick, and Yes or No to circle. Similar procedures are followed by public health centres and social welfare agencies. Staff members working in these institutions remain unaware of the aspirations of the family, their social networks, their economic activities, and their cultural habits. They know very little about family members' roles and relationships with each other, and how they might support or inhibit the care required by the young child. A teacher may not know, for example, that a parent who works three jobs may not be able to take her child to the local library or afford music lessons. A public health nurse may not know that some parents do not know how to search the internet for a physiotherapy clinic near their home, or how to ask someone in English or French for what they are looking for. The problem with the absence of such information is that the gap in information gets filled up either with the assumption that families served by the service providers are the same as their own, or that they fit the stereotypes that they have acquired through insufficient and distorted information.

In the following chapter three particular circumstances of disadvantage of families are discussed in some detail. These are not the only circumstances that disadvantage Canadian families, but we have selected them as they reflect our research interests and areas of expertise.

However, it is important to note that some of the experiences of families that have these disadvantages may be similar to families who have other disadvantages. For example, native families, same-sex families, or racialized families often encounter the same kind of marginalization that newcomer families, those who live in poverty or those who have a child with a disability, face in Canadian society.

Families in Disadvantaged Circumstances

The three types of families selected for this project will be discussed at some length in this chapter. It is important to remember that the characterizations of these families may not apply to all newcomer families, or those who live in poverty, or have a child with a disability. These are simply patterns associated with them, based on research conducted by scholars. Individual families may display some or none of the features discussed below.

Families who are newcomers

> Friends? I don't know…I don't know…I can't just press my neighbour's door [bell] and say, Can you take care of my children for a while? Although we see each other and we talk… 'How are you? How are you?

Are the kids fine? Maybe like the snow time… Oh do you see the snow?'
You know we pass comments, and just casual… but not friends! (A newcomer mother)

According to the census data from 2006 about one in four
Canadians over the age of 15 years was born outside Canada (Statistics
Canada, 2008). Until the 1970s, most newcomers to Canada came
from European countries, and were relatively familiar with languages,
cultures and social institutions of the other European settlers who had
preceded them. In the last four decades, however, newcomers have
largely come from non-traditional sources, such as East and South Asia,
the former Soviet Union, South America, Africa and the Middle East.
As Canada continues to receive about 250,000 newcomers every year,
most of them in the child-bearing ages of 25-44 years, the population of
newcomers and their children is projected to steadily increase in the
future [See DVD: Families who are newcomers.]

Unlike the immigrants from European countries, recent newcomers,
especially women who are the primary care-givers of young children, are
often unfamiliar with English or French, the two official languages in
Canada. They also do not have the social networks, information access,
or financial resources to benefit from publicly funded services, including those designed to serve newcomers (Ali & Kilbride, 2004). Most
new newcomers to Canada experience a significant decline in occupational status and disposable incomes (Li, 1998, 2003; Reitz, 2001) and
familial supports (Liamputtong, 2001). The rapid reduction in their
social, emotional, cultural and financial resources, in combination with
the often impermeable structures and cultures of Canadian institutions,
leads to the loss of the parents' sense of self-efficacy in their parenting
role (Ali, 2008).

Writing about newcomer parenting in Israel, Roer-Strier (2001) pro-
poses that newcomer parents bring with them conceptual models of the
successful adult that have evolved through generations in their original
cultural contexts. This image of an "adaptive adult" influences what

they consider to be "a good child" and also the contextually logical strategies they use for raising children. When they migrate to a new country, they find that socialization agents in the receiving society, such as teachers and social workers, have different images of the adaptive adult and different acculturation strategies for children. Newcomer parents and service professionals are usually unaware of these differences, but they can lead to tensions between them, and create internal conflicts for the child who is being cared for by both. Roer-Strier illustrates this phenomenon using the example of differences in newcomer parents' interpretations of child abuse and those of staff in child protection agencies. When such conflicts arise, she claims, "The parents are often left with a sense of helplessness" (p.239).

In Canada, as in other Western newcomer-receiving countries, notions about good parenting have evolved through discourses among white, European-origin policy-makers, academics, service providers, media professionals, and others who influence public opinion. These "regimes of truth" (Foucault, 1980) get accepted in society as the 'normal' and therefore the desirable ways of doing things (MacNaughton, 2005), which in turn frame public policy, institutional practices and individual decision-making. For example, young children in many Western societies are encouraged to learn to eat by themselves as soon as they can, but toilet training is delayed until they are about two or three years old. In other parts of the world children are fed by mothers and grandmothers even when they are capable of eating by themselves, but toilet training begins much earlier. Newcomer parents who are made to feel they are incompetent because they do not raise their children according to Western norms begin to lose confidence in their parenting abilities (Ali, 2008). They abandon the child-rearing strategies they are familiar with and try to emulate what they consider to be the superior Western ones. Critical theorist bell hooks calls this the "ideology of white supremacy" and post-colonial scholar Edward Said (1978) traces the origins of this kind of thinking to power relations based on the colonization of the East by the West, sustained through neo-colonial economic, political and socio-cultural relations. Criticizing the lack of newcomers' voices in influential positions, Razack (1998) claims that multiculturalism in Canada allows us to maintain "the fiction of equality" (p.60) by allowing newcomers to maintain the exotic aspects of their culture for the entertainment of Western consumers, but denying them access to power and privilege.

García Coll and her colleagues (see García Coll *et al.,* 1996; García Coll & Szalacha, 2004) emphasize the need to articulate specific contextual variables such as social class, race, and ethnicity in the analyses of experiences of 'minority' families, including newcomers, in Western societies. They claim that experiences that are not shared with the mainstream populations, such as racism and discrimination, and social, economic, and psychological segregation define the unique developmental pathways of racialized children. They argue that the social stratification of individuals and groups mediates the effects of other environmental factors. However, children and families are not passive recipients of these experiences. Their characteristics and the processes they use to interact with these systems contribute to their own socialization. Families of these children can help to reduce or magnify the effects of their social stratification.

The critical role of newcomer families in mediating the influence of the external environment on their children has been reiterated by several Canadian researchers as well. Beiser and colleagues (2002) claim that Canada's multiculturalism policy, designed to contribute to familial social capital, is only partially realized, at best. They suggest that, "Despite rules and guidelines to obviate it, delegitimizing of newcomer families' social and cultural capital by dominant-society institutions such as schools erode the families' protective potential and create emotional conflict for children." (p.226). They suggest that newcomer parents sometimes become overwhelmed with immigration-related stress, which also reduces their capacity to act as role models for their children. Seat (2003) tells us that newcomer youth who do not regard their parents as role models because they are depressed, confused, or overwhelmed by problems are at risk of developing negative and destructive values by identifying with other role models. Furthermore, Aycan and Kanungo (1998), based on their study of Indo-Canadian families, claim that "parents who preferred integration had children who also preferred integration. This was also the case for separation, assimilation, and marginalization." (p.465). A recent study conducted by Reitz and Banerjee (2007), based on the large scale Ethnic Diversity Survey, shows that visible minority children of newcomers believe there is a high level of racial discrimination, and have a great sense of alienation, in Canadian society. This study was based on several indicators of social cohesion such as sense of belonging in Canada, trust in others, self-identification as Canadians, acquisition of citizenship, life satisfaction, volunteering, and voting patterns.

Families living in poverty

> Poverty has an emotional impact because it feels like outside forces control your life, such as landlords, and government agencies. You feel vulnerable and ashamed asking for assistance whether it be at the food bank or daycare subsidy. (A mother living in poverty)

There is a considerable body of research demonstrating that low family income can put healthy child development at risk, either directly by limiting the resources parents can use for creating a safe, healthy, and stimulating environment for the child, or indirectly by reducing parents' capacity to provide supportive and consistent parenting as a result of poverty-related stress (Evans, 1995; Hertzman, 2002; Levin, 1995; Rothman, 2007; Schissel & Wotherspoon, 2001; Schorr 1988). [See DVD: Families living in poverty.]

The study of poverty in Canada is hindered by a lack of consensus on its definition. According to Kerr and Beaujot (2003), the official position is that Statistics Canada does not, and indeed cannot, measure the level of poverty because of a lack of agreement among Canadians on how poverty can best be defined. In practice, though, Statistics Canada's Low Income Cut-Off rate (LICO), which is primarily a taxation measure, continues to be the most widely used indicator of poverty in the media and in popular discussions of social policy. In general, this indicator is based on the cost of living in different parts of the country and the number of people dependent on the family income. This figure obviously changes on the basis of inflation rates, movement within the country, and other factors.

Although Canada does not have a government-approved definition of poverty, it does not mean that there is no poverty in Canada. Statistics Canada has determined that families who spend more than 55% of their income on food, shelter and clothing are living in poverty (Campaign 2000, Defining Poverty 2003). Campaign 2000 (2008) has recently estimated that there are 760,000 children, which is one out of every nine children, who live in poverty in Canada.

Children born into poverty are more likely to be born prematurely or of low birth weight. They are more likely to drop out of school, and therefore are also less likely to be employed and support themselves when they are adults. Evans (1995) points out that poverty continues to be the most persistent predictor of both low achievement in and dropping out from school and low income in adulthood. Poverty forces children to live in neighbourhoods where violence, crime, drug abuse, and other anti-social practices are very common. Early and continuing exposure to these practices makes them more likely to emulate such behaviours as they grow older. Children who live in poverty may also suffer from poor nutrition, inadequate health care, overcrowded and unsafe housing, lack of appropriate role models, insufficient educational support at home (Levin, 1995; Schissel & Wotherspoon, 2001), and low levels of vision, hearing, speech, mobility, dexterity, and cognitive and emotional competence (Campaign 2000, Defining Poverty 2003). Schorr (1988) has identified poverty and lack of social supports for parents as factors that impede children's social integration. In fact, the prevalence of poverty in urban neighbourhoods has been linked to poor developmental outcomes in children. In a Vancouver study entire sections of the city include children at higher risks of developing multiple problems in physical health, social competence, emotional maturity, and communication skills because of poverty, crime and violence that tend to coalesce in certain neighbourhoods (Hertzman, 2002).

A widely held perception in Canada is that the presence of at least one employed adult in the family is an indication that the family does not live in poverty. However, this is often not the case. People who work for low wages often cannot afford adequate housing, appropriate clothing or sufficient healthy food for their families. Some of them even work two or three jobs, and risk neglecting their child-care responsibilities to maximize their working hours, but still cannot make enough to provide a decent living standard for their family.

Research suggests that the longer a child lives in poverty, the more lasting its impact. Children who live in poverty for a long period of time are more likely to fail to meet developmental benchmarks than those who live in poverty for a short period of time (Evans, 1995). The National Longitudinal Study of Children and Youth (NLSCY) is a long-term study by Social Development Canada and Statistics Canada that follows the development of children from birth to early adulthood, assessing children's development every two years. The study began in 1994 with a large sample of children under the age of 12. Researchers working on this study collect information about factors that influence the social, emotional, and behavioural development of children, and monitor the impact of these factors on their development over time. The evidence collected so far shows that a family's socio-economic status is closely associated with children's well-being, school achievement, and behavioural patterns.

The Organisation for Economic Co-operation and Development (OECD) estimates that 15% to 30% of children and youth in its member nations are at risk of failing to complete school and therefore experiencing subsequent problems of integration into labour markets and adult life (Evans, 1995, pp. 25-27; Evans & Hurrell, 1996, pp. 19-20).

Crucial factors associated with risk status include poverty, ethnic minority status, community or family characteristics such as single parent status, parents' education, inadequate housing, child abuse, home-school breakdown, inadequate knowledge of official languages, and type and geographic location of schools (Evans, 1995). One of the most serious concerns expressed by communities who see themselves poorly served by schools—including residents in some rural regions and Aboriginal people in diverse communities—is the failure of education systems to connect with the lives and worlds of the learners they are meant to serve (DeYoung, 1994; Royal Commission on Aboriginal Peoples, 1996).

Because children's ability to benefit from public services is crucially dependent on their families' values, priorities, resources, and strategies for seeking and using support systems, service providers in health, education, recreation, and other social services need to take into account these families' particular circumstances to help 'level the playing field' for the children who live in disadvantaged circumstances. According to Turnbull and colleagues (2007), staff in service organizations who actively listen to families, focusing on how and what to offer, are more effective in linking them with the supports and services they actually want and need. In doing so, they also "honour parents' choices, involve multiple family members, build on family strengths, establish partnerships, and collaborate with families in individualized and flexible ways" (Turnbull *et al.*, 2007, p. 188).

Families with a child with a disability

"I've noticed that people who first meet my oldest son in a wheelchair...they hesitate...because you know...unfortunately the stigma...the leper stigma still goes on with disabilities...." (Father of a son with Duchenne muscular dystrophy)

The identification of a child at birth or in early childhood as having a disability (such as Down syndrome, autism, hearing loss or cerebral palsy) is a difficult discovery for any family. In Canada, an estimated 5-7% of children and youth have disabilities (Canadian Association for Community Living, 2008). According to Statistics Canada this means that about 155,000 Canadian children between ages 5-14 have a disability. Although families with a child with a disability do not necessarily perceive the experience as negative (Abbot & Meredith, 1986), Scott, Sexton and Wood (1986) suggest that the stress level of families of children with disabilities is generally higher than for families with typically developing children. The responsibility of raising a child with a disability poses additional challenges to families. Stress levels are compounded when parents have to find appropriate resources and intervention services, devote extra time to care for the child, attend doctor and therapist appointments, and cope with the increased financial costs of meeting the child's needs. This increased stress often stretches the family's coping capabilities, which in turn negatively affects the entire family, including the child with the disability, as well as other children. This makes it imperative that family stressors be assessed as part of planning with the family for appropriate intervention services (Lessenberry & Rehfeldt, 2004; Xu, 2007). [See DVD: Families with a child with a disability.]

Most parents of children with disabilities report that their child's needs are unmet (Statistics Canada, Children with Disabilities and Their Families, 2003). According to this report, of the 155,000 children with disabilities only 8.8% reported that they received formal help from government organizations or agencies. Among parents of the 39,000 children with severe to very severe disabilities who required help for their care, 69% indicated that they did not receive all the help they needed. Among parents of the 13,000 children with mild to moderate disabilities whose parents required help, 55% said they did not receive all the help they needed. Thirty-six percent (36%) of these parents reported that they did not know where to look for help. In most cases (65%) only mothers provide the care for the child with the disability. Fathers exclusively care for only 3% of such children, while both parents care for them in 30% of the cases.

The need to care for a child with a disability also has a significant impact on family employment. When mothers care for a child with a disability they either do not work outside the home, or limit their employment to fewer hours or less demanding work. Based on their extensive survey of postal workers in Canada whose children have disabilities, Irwin and Lero (2004) found that 90% of the families reported stress in balancing their work and family life. Furthermore, many families were unable to maintain employment due to lack of appropriate and affordable child care for their children. Trute and Hiebert-Murphy (2007) also found that 48% of the 103 Canadian families they interviewed, who had a child with a disability, could also be classified as "low-income households" (p.112). Thus families having a child with a disability also constitute a disproportionate number of those who live in poverty because they are unable to generate sufficient income.

> My situation is more financial. I remember when they handed me the first bill for Carl's prosthetic, going, "Oh my God, it is $8,000 for this piece of plastic!" (Mother of a child with a physical disability)

There is now sufficient evidence to suggest that inclusive, early, and family-centred interventions are effective in ameliorating the effects of the child's disability and improving prospects for the child's life experiences (Odom, 2000). However, when a family is from a different cultural, ethnic or linguistic background than the service provider, early intervention and education services do not always match the values, priorities, expectations and needs of the family (Xu, 2007). Effective communication between service providers and families is more difficult, which leads to mistrust, misunderstandings, and frustration on both sides. Lai and Ishiyama (2004) found that Chinese-Canadian mothers of children with disabilities perceived their stress in adapting to a new environment, limited proficiency in English, and differing beliefs about teaching and learning as barriers to their full involvement in their children's care and education. These findings underscore the importance of using a family empowerment model in which service providers strive to understand the priorities, beliefs, and aspirations of the family while collaborating with them in the adaptation of their services or creation of new ones (Turnbull, Turbiville & Turnbull, 2000).

> The teacher is a lovely lady but she has...she has 22 kids in her class besides the two boys (with disabilities)...so we really don't communicate with her too much because I think she relies upon her E.A. (Father of a child included in a grade 1 class)

Other reasons why children with disabilities and their families do not receive the services they need include insufficient teacher training, inadequate funding, and limited specialized resources (Frankel, 2004; Irwin, Lero & Brophy, 2000). While not all of these issues can be addressed immediately or adequately, they can be better understood and prioritized through a respectful, ongoing dialogue between service providers and families who have a child with a disability.

The Narrative Approach

A narrative is any cohesive and coherent story with an identifiable beginning, middle, and end that provides information about scene, characters, and conflict; raises unanswered questions or unresolved conflict; and provides resolution. (Hinyard & Kreuter, 2007, p.778)

While there is no consensus in the literature on the term 'narrative' (Hinyard & Kreuter, 2007; Riessman & Quinney, 2005), our use of this term fits well with the above definition proposed by Hinyard and Kreuter, who also call it "the basic mode of human interaction and a fundamental way of acquiring knowledge" (p. 777). They remind us that telling of and listening to narratives is an old and well-established form of communication in which information about situations and events is provided with descriptive details for the purpose of learning and teaching. [See DVD: Introduction: The narrative approach.]

Connelly and Clandinin (1988) have revived the use of narratives as a tool for research. They claim that narratives provide a way of understanding how individuals draw on their personal practical knowledge to understand life's situations. They suggest that our views about our world are derived from our personal, historical, and socio-cultural narratives, and play a central role in defining our everyday realities. Thus a narrative structures the way we act in the present, and can guide our future practices. Similarly, Fiese and Spagnola (2005), and Rossiter (1999) suggest that narratives provide individuals with greater understanding of the past and the future.

> Narratives are a reflection of how the individual or family organizes representations of social exchanges, has learned from the past, and anticipates the future (Fiese & Spagnola, 2005, p. 52).

When people are asked to recount important events personally, they give new meanings to the events as they recreate their circumstances, struggles, and resolutions (Fiese & Spagnola, 2005). Narrating experiences enables people to elaborate and reflect upon their significance, which is much more useful than just the factual information (Bochner, 2001). This reflective process is particularly beneficial when considering matters of "morality, religion, personal values, meaning in a person's life, [and] complex social relationships..." (Hinyard & Kreuter, 2007, p. 778). In the creation of their narratives, the narrators gain deeper insight into their life's experiences, and how they interpret those experiences. As Rossiter (1999) suggests, narratives are a "means through which humans make meaning of experience" (p. 62) as the course of their life continues to develop and change. Narratives may also generate a sense of conviction, as the narrators begin to convey their beliefs, values, and responsibilities (Navarro, 2003).

Narratives are also a mechanism for creating a dialogue that could illuminate diverse perspectives on the same issue (Shields, 2004). The sharing of stories through narratives can give greater meaning to our own lives, as well as in the ways we perceive the lives of others (Skott,

2001). They offer us a chance to explore and share our beliefs, relationships and experiences (Hendry 2007). They allow us to compare with others the interpretation of our experiences through ethical, emotional, and practical lenses (Bochner, 2001). Those who listen to others' narratives also gain insights into the narrators' understandings of their world, particularly about how they make sense of testing times of hardship and unsettled emotions (Fies & Spagnola, 2005).

Several scholars (Navarro, 2003; Rossiter, 1999; and Squire, 2005) have suggested that narratives both express and influence our identity as they not only provide information about the world in which we live, but also about who we are, and how we place ourselves in this world. What people choose to include in the telling of their narrative, the claims they make about their lives, the relationship they develop with the audience, and their stance as protagonists or victims, help to shape their identity (Navarro, 2003).

Although the terms 'narrative' and 'story' are sometimes used interchangeably, Fiese and Spagnola (2005) recommend that the subtle distinction between them be maintained. They suggest that the term narrative acknowledges that people selectively choose, elaborate, and interpret information in the creation of their narratives. This is different from simply recounting a story, which is limited to the content and structure of recalled experience. Following their advice, we will use the term narrative in this book as inclusive of the process of making sense of an event or personal experience by the narrator.

Family narratives

Narratives afford the opportunity to examine implicit and sometimes unexamined beliefs that families hold about relationships and critical events. Family narratives reflect how the family makes sense of its world, how the family expresses rules of interaction, and the trustworthiness of relationships. (Fiese & Spagnola, 2005, p. 51)

Listening to life stories of families informs service providers in the fields of early care and education, health, and other social services with crucial information about the families, which can help them to tailor their services to meet the families' needs. It is a less exploitative way to access and acknowledge the experiences of those who are conventionally disadvantaged in society (Hendry, 2007, p.489). This approach challenges service providers to engage with families as collaborators, to adapt their practices to harmonize with the family's expectations and priorities, and to create synergy for new service possibilities. Rather than viewing families as needy, uninformed, and disempowered, we can use the narrative approach to emphasize the resilience, optimism, and other strengths of families.

Listening to family narratives often leads to change in the relationship between the listener and the family participating in the interview process. There is a shift from a focus on general information toward the personal and particular, which in turn opens the way for understanding alternative ways of knowing and doing (Clandinin, 2007). Service providers who listen to family narratives begin to see possibilities that could transform their approach to practice in order to better meet the needs of the particular family. Five principal characteristics of the narrative approach make this possible:

The narrative approach is holistic. Thus the narrative approach allows the listener to view families in all of their complexity, rather than to focus on one distinct aspect of the family. The family has many individual characteristics that extend beyond its newcomer status, its poverty, or its child's disabilities. For example, a mother may be viewed by a nutritionist as resistant to providing her child with healthy meals, while it is her poor self-image, limited funds, or minimal choice at the food bank that make it difficult for her to do so. Or, a teacher may focus exclusively on promoting the reading skills of a child with Down syndrome, but not appreciate that the family wants to focus on the child's gross motor development so he will be able to play in the neighbourhood playground with other children.

The narrative approach is authentic. The power of family narratives lies in its authentic representation of the narrators' voices. When members of a family narrate and reflect upon their experiences, exercising greater control over what they choose to disclose and how they make sense of those disclosures, the chances of distortion or inappropriate interpretation are reduced. These narratives represent actual families and are more accurate and meaningful representations of families than the composites that are sometimes created by educators as 'cases' for instructional purposes, which may highlight some features of families but neglect others. When families are provided the opportunity to review and edit their narratives, it further ensures that their true voices come through.

The narrative approach gives voice to the family. Family narratives provide a unique opportunity to give voice to families, particularly to those who are different in significant ways from the dominant groups in a society who conceptualize, monitor and evaluate, and offer public services designed for all families. Such families are usually neglected in the design of service provisions because institutional structures and cultures do not permit their meaningful participation in decision-making processes. In the school system, for example, newcomer parents do not participate actively in school councils because their lack of fluency in the official language or unfamiliarity with the culture shared by the group is often interpreted as incompetence by other members of the group. Similarly, parents of children with disabilities who simply cannot find the time to participate in meetings may be considered uninterested in their child's education. Because the development of family narratives is an individualized process, factors such as the language used or timing of the narration are based on the family's genuine availability, preference or convenience.

The narrative approach creates synergy. The development of a family narrative often creates synergy between the family and the service provider who listens to and documents the narrative. Families are challenged to reflect on their life and create new meanings of their experiences, while the listeners are challenged to reconsider their assumptions about the 'type' of family they are engaging with. As new, more nuanced understandings are developed of what individual families are like, ideas emerge for new ways of serving them.

The narrative approach can be transformative. For many families, the creation of their narrative is a transformative experience because as they construct their narrative, they give new meaning to past events, see their relationships from another perspective, articulate previously un-stated beliefs, and find some coherence in their lives. The allocation of time, space, and an empathic, non-judgmental listener allows them to recognize their strengths and identify strategies they have found effective in reaching their goals. The distance provided by the act of constructing a narrative allows them to review their past and formulate new goals. At the same time service providers begin to see the fullness and complexity of a family's life instead of seeing members in uni-dimensional ways, that is, simply as clients, patients, or parents of a child they work with.

Possibilities and limitations

The development of narratives is a lengthy and labour intensive process, as it often involves interviewing, transcribing and analyzing the information provided by the families (Fiese & Spagnola, 2005), followed by the construction of narratives that are representative and true to the families' accounts. However, the creation of a narrative is an intimate, "meaning-making" process (Fiese & Spagnola, 2005, p. 51) that provides deeper insights into the perceptions and perspectives of the families. Through the use of narratives, families are offered a chance to explore and share their own beliefs, relationships, and experiences. This allows service providers insights into how families understand and perceive the world, and how they make sense of their everyday lives.

Bochner (2001) argues that the main crux of the narrative approach is not to reiterate only the facts, but also to express the meaning and importance of these experiences. Shields (2004) explains that facts alone do not generate understanding, but rather it is the ability to collate one's experiences and realities which influences the meaning- making process. Similarly, Rossiter (1999) argues that narratives maintain a meaning-making component intended to evoke greater understanding of life and experience, rather than to deliver facts, logic, predictability, and control (p. 61). Therefore, the importance of knowledge gained through narratives is that it stimulates rich insight and deeper learning, rather than "an objective and dispassionate depiction of the world" (Beattie et al., 2007, p. 122).

The danger of the narrative approach is that it may deconstruct the information collected into "a series of events, categories, or themes" in which the researcher weaves together these pieces and entitles it as a narrative (Hendry, 2007, p. 491). Hendry asserts that this way of developing the narrative can eliminate important portions of the shared experiences. Thus, the narratives become fragmented.

Narratives that explore life stories and experiences are susceptible to the 'lifting practice' in which interviewers disassemble the written narratives, and highlight only selected segments of the story. Consequently, such a practice abandons the overall essence of the story (Adams, 2008). Yet, as Salmon asserts, "All narratives are...co-constructed. The audience [researcher], whether physically present or not, exerts a crucial influence on what can and cannot be said, how things should be expressed, what can be taken for granted, what needs explaining, and so on." (cited in Riessman & Quinney, 2005, p. 399).

Hendry (2007) cautions researchers from attributing "preconceived notions" (p. 493) to the narrative in order to suit personal beliefs and knowledge. As Adams (2008) notes, it is possible to keep such attribution in check by careful reflection on how our prior knowledge and experiences may influence our interpretation and representation of someone else's narrative. Furthermore, Beattie *et al.* (2007) assert that interpretations of narratives should ideally be a mutual activity, involving both the interviewer and participant. In this case, both parties engage in the reconstructing of meaning in the narrative. Beattie *et al.* state,

As researchers and participants negotiate meanings and co-create understandings, they acknowledge their temporal quality, and recognize that they are subject to ongoing interpretation and reconstruction. The meanings and knowledge made through shared interpretation and meaning-making is inter-subjective in that it represents both the researcher's and practitioner's perspectives, understandings, and voices (p. 122).

When interpreting narratives, researchers [or service providers] must also acknowledge the cultural context in which a story is recounted (Navarro, 2003). Narratives reside within particular "familial, religious, socio-economic and cultural contexts" (Rossiter, 1999, p. 65). Navarro (2003) states that stories are "told under particular social conditions and constraints; historical, institutional, and biographical contexts" (p. 129). Narratives that take into account the social and cultural contexts enhance the overall "intelligibility, believability, and relevance of stories" (Navarro, 2003, p. 129); they make sense when being considered within a shared cultural understanding (Rossiter, 1999).

Narratives explore the roles culture and society play in shaping one's life and *vice versa*; they may be perceived as a "cultural trace" (Squire, 2005, p. 103). Similarly, Skott (2001) suggests that narratives have the ability to portray "the process of culture creation as it is taking place" (p.253). For example, in her book *Sweatshop Warriors*, Ching Yoon Louie describes the experiences of minority newcomer women within the United States (as cited in Navarro, 2003). Louie's use of narratives explores the women's reasons for coming to America and the realities of existing as sweatshop workers within the U.S. The narratives within *Sweatshop Warriors* illuminate "the voices of working-class leaders thinking through their situations and the strategies necessary to improve their lives" (Navarro, 2003, p. 132). The narratives were a powerful means of "binding" people together through sharing common experiences, shaping identities, and eventually stimulating action (Navarro, 2003, p. 138).

Finally, the use of narratives has been criticized for the loss of emotional content and sensitivity that sometimes results when attributing words to the experience (Squire, 2005). Words expressed within a narrative cannot always illustrate the unprocessed emotions of one's experience, as sometimes the emotions may "fall outside words" (p. 102). For example, emotions such as grief, loss, embarrassment, or disgrace may never be fully represented within a narrative.

Developing the
Narratives

The art of listening is indispensable with the right use of the mind. It is also the most gracious, the most open and the most generous of human habits. (Krames, 2002, p. 56)

Listening to families has been advocated in the helping professions for a long time, under the general approach of family-centred practice. It is included as a part of best practices in the field of early intervention, care, and education (Trivette and Dunst, 2005). Individual narratives have also been used in nursing (Skott, 2001), social work (Riessman & Quincy, 2005), and other health related professions (Hinyard & Kreuter, 2007) to promote behavioural change. However, in most cases the information requested from families is brief and perfunctory, meant only to acknowledge families' perspectives but not to understand them, designed to change families' behaviours but not our own beliefs and practices. For example, Beckman, Newcomb,

Frank, and Brown (1996) identify three stepping stones to building positive family-centred practice: acknowledging the family's competence in taking leadership in a child's life, acknowledging the family's wish to do the best for its child, and respecting the family's beliefs and feelings by communicating this understanding to family members. Similarly, Dunst and colleagues (1988) talk about listening to families for effective provision of guidance, treatment, and support by "truly understanding the needs and concerns of help seekers, being responsive to what is important to help seekers, and promoting acquisition of competencies that permit help seekers to become better able to manage life events and negotiate their developmental courses" (Dunst *et al.*, 1988, p. 74).

What is unique about what we propose here is the breadth and depth of the guiding questions, the details included, and the systematic, collaborative way in which information is collected, compiled, and edited. Values, aspirations, beliefs and histories are included in the kind of family narratives we suggest, as they help to put current contexts in perspective and locate the reasons for families' actions and decisions. We recommend that the interviews be conducted over three or four sessions that they are at least an hour long, audio-taped, and then fully transcribed. They can be conducted with either one or more than one family member at a time, as long as there is sufficient opportunity for each person to be fully heard. Furthermore, we strongly recommend that families be interviewed by service providers themselves rather than by hired researchers, and that they write the narratives in collaboration with the families they serve. This is because the primary purpose of listening to families is to enable service providers to reflect upon their institutional and personal practices from the perspectives of families they are supposed to serve, particularly those who have typically been marginalized in our societies. [See DVD: Resources: Simulations of narrative interviews.]

Undeniably, families who collaborate with service providers in developing their narratives feel empowered. This helps to create the synergy between them and their service provider, which can be channelled into unique actions and services for family support (Turnbull, Turbiville, & Turnbull, 2000). This change, however, evolves slowly as families and service providers build trust and jointly devise new ways to meet the goals, values, priorities and needs of the family. Professionals must start by considering their own values and life priorities and try to learn more about those of the families they serve. It is important to remember that people's values find expressions in different ways. Common values may be reflected in different behaviours, and similar behaviour may be based on very different values.

The quality of interactions between the service provider and the family during an engagement in developing narratives plays a crucial role in the nature and depth of information that is shared. It is critical that listening skills, interviewing techniques, and methods of recording be mastered by the service provider in order to utilize the powerful tool of listening to the family's life experiences without distraction (McKeown *et al.*, 2006). Effective narrative interviewers are deeply committed to uninterrupted listening to the voice of the speaker, showing empathy, providing prompts where necessary, and honouring silences where needed. Those who are skilled in this work manage to give the speaker "a sensation that there is someone who does not want anything other than to listen to her life narrative" (Vajda, 2007, p.89). [See DVD: Developing the narratives.]

Ethical considerations

Before you can approach any family to collect information about them, you will need to get formal approval from your organization to do this work. Many large organizations already have forms and processes in place for this. However, in case your organization does not have these, you will need to write an application and get formal approval from senior managers or a designated committee. The purpose of this approval is to protect the rights of those who provide the information you gather. It helps to ensure that you, or other people who have access to the information you collect, will not harm or violate the privacy of the people who provided it, knowingly or unknowingly.

The formal approval is required for you to begin to approach families you want to talk to. Once your plan for how you will select and approach the families has been approved by your organization, you can contact the families to seek their approval to participate in your work. This usually requires a written agreement (see Appendix III for an example), which is supplemented by verbal explanations. The agreement usually includes details such as the ways in which their privacy will be protected, the different forms and purposes for which the information will be used, who will have access to it, whether the interviews will be audio-taped or not, whether the interviewees will be compensated for their time or not, and what they could do in case their rights are not respected. The purpose of this agreement is to make sure the participants fully understand what they are agreeing to, and in some cases the forms may need to be translated, orally or in writing.

Our perspective is that ethical considerations in developing family narrative go well beyond the formal processes of approvals for information collection by your organization and the families themselves. Ethical conduct in this work ranges from respectful and non-judgmental engagement with the families during the period in which you interview them, to faithful transcription of the interviews, multiple readings of the transcripts to identify key themes, and complete attention to making sure the families' voices are fully and accurately represented in the narratives while their privacy is being respected. Further details on how you might try to do all this are in the following sections. [See DVD: Using the narratives.]

Approaching families

In approaching families to take part in the creation of narratives, it is important to let them know the purpose the narratives will serve in their lives. Explain how valuable it is for service providers to know them as they really are, with all their hopes for themselves and their children. Discuss how services they may need could be improved, based on their experiences in the past, and your own experience as a service provider. You may want to give them an example of a time when you only learned afterwards of some key piece of information that would have allowed you to serve a family better. Assure them of the confidentiality of the information they provide, and let them know that you will not use that information for purposes other than what you have both agreed upon. Point out that at the end of the process of creating a narrative, they will have a document that they can provide to each new teacher, health clinic, or other service provider who will be working with them and their children.

Service providers who participated in this project told us that they were initially concerned about approaching families to ask for their narratives. They felt the families might consider it intrusive, or might not want to commit several hours of their time over the three or four sessions of interviews. However, they were surprised by the enthusiastic reception to their proposal, and the sustained interest in continuing the work. Many families invited them to their homes, and genuinely welcomed the opportunity to have an empathic, non-judgmental person listen to them with attention and respect. They expressed appreciation for the fact that someone was listening to their whole story with an interest in their past, present, and future, and not just a fragment of their life such as their child's behaviour, or the family's need for new housing.

Engaging families

Jerry, Elaine, George, and Kramer in the widely popular television show Seinfeld teach us the power of talking about the seemingly mundane daily minutia of our lives as a way of connecting with and engaging other people. Meeting a family for the first time at a coffee house, at the neighbourhood playground, or in their kitchen allows for discussions about the weather, their baby's first smile, or a new food bank they have discovered. This 'small talk' offers us glimpses into the lives other people lead – their values, their priorities, and their dreams. It is a first step towards understanding the context of a family's life. It demonstrates that you are truly interested in what they have to say and engages the family in wanting to tell their life story. These informal interactions, which include positive eye contact, active listening, and attention to families' emotions, are paramount to developing rapport with the family (Eggenberger and Nelms, 2007).

Interactions with the family should be located in an environment that is physically comfortable, emotionally supportive, and non-judgmental. For some families the family home is the best setting in which to disclose their aspirations, feelings, and needs. For other families a neutral setting outside the home or an office where there are no other distractions is more suitable. This environment must be quiet and private to protect the confidentiality of the speaker. The critical condition is that the interviewer is attentive, and the speakers are able to express themselves free of concerns about interruptions or lack of privacy.

We strongly recommend that you plan to audio-tape the interviews and also take brief notes (which you should expand as soon as possible right after the interview). The audiotapes will allow you to record exactly what was said, and enable you to listen to that again. The initial notes will help you record the tenor of your conversation by making notes about non-verbal expressions of feelings such as anxiety, joy, boredom, or grief. As it is difficult to maintain eye contact and write at the same time, it is important that you expand your notes into readable, more detailed descriptions about your interviews immediately afterwards.

Our experience in developing family narratives tells us that in most cases only one adult member of the family, usually a woman, is available and willing to be interviewed 3-4 times by a service provider. Under optimal conditions it should be possible to interview all members of the family over a longer period of time. In our project we only planned to interview the adults in the family, and found it difficult to reach more than one of them in most cases. If more than one adult in a family is willing to participate in your work, we suggest that you interview them together on one occasion, but no more than that. It is important to also interview them separately so that you can listen to their different voices, which may get interrupted or overshadowed in a joint interview. [See DVD: Developing the Narratives – Engaging families.]

Finding the 'I' in communication

Deborah Tannen (1990), social linguist and author, describes communication as occurring at both the level of the "message" and the level of the "metamessage". At the level of the message we convey our meaning through words we use to communicate with someone, such as "I need to see you for…." At the level of the metamessage, however, important information is communicated through roles, settings, facial expressions, and body language that qualifies, elaborates, and contextualizes the verbal information. This information identifies the nature of the relationship between the two people in conversation – who has power, who is more competent, who is concerned about whom and why. Individuals receiving these metamessages interpret the information based on their own cultural and social experiences and react accordingly. Some nonverbal communications, such as the nod of a head, a touch on the arm or silence can signal engagement and empathy. Others such as a vacant look can convey boredom. A setting in which one person is clearly comfortable while the other person is not signals a hierarchical relationship. Early in your planning, you therefore need to take the time to plan how to seek feedback and reflect on your own personal communication style, and think about how to analyze metamessages you may inadvertently convey to the family whose narrative you want to create.

This does not mean that you should try to erase your personal style from the interaction, or pretend that your own values, assumptions, or choice of words and gestures will not influence the conversations. It is impossible to remove the self from any interaction, and all interactions are shaped by reciprocal engagement. However, it is possible to strive to give greater control to the family being interviewed to choose what they want to talk about and how. Encouraging interviewees to bring in the 'I' more often in their talk is likely to yield more in-depth information about their feelings, thoughts, and attitudes.

Questions that guide, not lead

Questions are always central to any interview, but in the narrative approach the lead is taken by the interviewee, while the interviewer simply guides the discussion to help unfold the history, emotions, and attitudes of the interviewees. Let the interviewees emphasize things important to them, and use questions to encourage them to elaborate and clarify a topic under discussion. Comments such as the following are often helpful

- "Tell me more about that."
- "Can you give me an example of …."
- "How do you feel about that now?"
- "Is there anything else you want to add?"

While we have provided an interview guide (see Appendix II: Interview guidelines) to suggest questions you may want to ask, it is by no means a prescriptive list of questions. It is intended to be used flexibly, modified according to the leads provided by the family, the nature of your relationship, and the kind of information that may be most pertinent in your professional context.

Listening actively

The ability to convey empathy to the family requires your full attention, active responses and even your silence. By actively listening to the family's life experiences, service providers validate the family's history as important, and show their appreciation for the gift of the information they give them.

Communicating with families
- Listen to the family's story with empathy while reserving judgment
- Learn about the family's strengths, resources, values, and priorities
- Respect cultural diversity and parental aspirations for success
- Share information, resources, and decision-making
  Adapted from Frankel & Gold (2007)

We agree with Vajda's recommendation (2007) that interviewers refrain from interrupting the interview with comments or questions such as: "And you did not think that....?" or "Did you not feel that ....?" or the even more invasive question "Don't you have ....?" or "Why didn't you ....?" as these may make the interviewees feel as if they are being blamed. Rather, nonjudgmental responses and questions which encourage families to illustrate their ideas with examples, or provide greater details about events and experiences, should be employed. [See DVD: Resources – Simulation.]

Mirroring: One way to show empathy and engagement is to mirror words, tone, and body language used by the person being interviewed. By repeating a key phrase or idea that the family member tells you in your own words, the interviewer is not only showing interest but is acknowledging the importance of this thought and allowing the speaker to reflect on it. This allows the speaker to expand, correct, or adjust the intent of the message and your understanding of the words. If a person says in a strong voice, "The schools in Canada don't have children show respect to their elders," you might say with a similar strong tone, "You think schools in Canada do not teach children to respect their elders." The interviewee can then consider the words you have reflected back and modify to explain, "The schools in Canada are different from the schools in my country. I would like to see respect for elders clearly taught in schools."

Acknowledging feelings: The interviewer can show compassion for the interviewee's feelings by verbalizing the emotion conveyed by the non-verbal messages given by body language. This is another way to show understanding of what the other person is experiencing without judging. For example, if a mother seems to be wringing her hands and tears are in her eyes while describing her child's medical condition, the interviewer can comment, "You seem very distressed by your child's medical condition," or, to show empathy, "This must be so distressing for you."

Self-disclosure: Empathy can also be communicated through brief, relevant disclosure about yourself and/or your family to demonstrate that you can understand and relate to the situation being described. Caution must be taken that you do not take over and shift the focus of attention to yourself. Remember it is the family's story which is central, not yours. If a family member discusses the challenges of putting her children to bed at night, you may simply say, "I remember similar difficulties with my children."

Honouring silences: Interviewees often need to review, consider and compose their thoughts and emotions before they speak. The interviewer may echo the last words of an answer or use nonverbal expressions such as a questioning look to encourage the interviewee to expand further on a thought. Respecting the silence, long as it may seem, is better than rushing to fill the seemingly empty space with a new question. The question may seem intrusive and be misconstrued as a lack of interest on the part of the interviewer in what the interviewee is thinking about or trying to articulate. Allow the family member the opportunity to reflect without your feeling the need to fill the silence. A simple "yes" or a filler such as "um" will go further to show you are still listening, are giving the speaker time to think, and are anticipating more details. [See DVD: Developing the narrative.]

Concluding the interview

At the end of each interview, summarize the key information, thoughts and feelings highlighted in the interview. This signals that you were really listening to the interviewee and provides an opportunity to correct any misunderstandings. This is an important step in assuring that the information used in formulating the family narrative reflects what the interviewee considers important to include. Plan for the next interview before you leave the family. When, where, and at what time will you meet again are all important collaborative decisions. The families must also be informed as to when they will receive a first written draft of the family narrative for their consideration (see below), and when and how they will participate in editing their narratives.

Writing the narrative with the family

The writing of the narratives is a demanding process. It involves transcribing the recorded conversations, picking out key themes and important quotations, weaving them into a coherent text, and then editing this text in collaboration with the family. It includes the following steps:

Transcribing audiotapes – Although this is a time-consuming process, we want to encourage you to do at least some of this work yourself, because listening to the tapes allows you to recall the emotional tenor of the conversation, and also allows you to reflect upon your interviewing skills. For the first few times, you should try to fully transcribe the interview, to see how you can hone your skills in guiding the conversation. Later, you can skip over the less relevant portions of your conversations.

Because this is the most time-consuming part of developing narratives, you may want to get voluntary or paid help in transcribing some of your interviews.

Analyzing transcripts and notes – Read over the transcribed interviews a few times, simply asking yourself: Who is this person, and what is important to him/her? Or who is this family and what is important to them? As you pick out the salient events of their lives, their important relationships, their views about how to raise their children, their particular values and strengths, and their aspirations and strategies, make notes for yourself about these. Write down significant quotes that illustrate any of these. Then try to knit together the information you have gleaned into a short (2-3 pages) text, including the significant quotes, which portrays the family as fully but also as concisely as you can. Try to keep your language simple, so that potential readers (other service providers and those who educate them, as well as the families whose narrative it is) can fully understand what is there.

Checking in with the family – Take the draft to the families and give them some time to read it on their own, reminding them that it is a first draft and that you will be revising it according to their direction. Then meet them again to ask: Does the narrative portray them accurately? Are there details they would like to change, add, or delete? Remind them of the potential readers of their narrative and ask them to choose pseudonyms for themselves and their communities, neighbourhoods or towns (if these are included in the narrative). If the families suggest any changes, incorporate them into the next version of the narrative and send it back to them for their final approval. Make sure you provide them copies of the narrative to keep for themselves, or to use in any way they want to, such as introducing themselves to their child's new teacher, or the public health nurse in their local clinic. Before you take leave of the families, it is important to show your gratitude for the gift of their narrative. [See DVD: Developing the narrative – The process.]

Using Narratives

We learned that every family has a story and until you know their background you can't really understand their behaviours or the reasons for their actions. Since learning more about [the family] we have changed our approach in working with them. We only wish we had the time to sit down with each and every one of our families to learn their stories, and we know this would help us when we design our programs. (Family Support Services staff member)

In this chapter we offer some examples of how service providers in different fields can develop and use family narratives to enhance their professional practice. We also suggest ways in which educators of pre-service and in-service professionals can use family narratives to develop a deeper understanding of families the students work with, or will work with. We summarize the benefits of developing and using family narratives, including the benefits for families who participate in this work.

We conclude with some questions that we are left with to stimulate further experimentation and research.

The accompanying DVD contains testimonials from persons who have worked in different public services, and are now in leadership positions in their fields, on the value of incorporating family narratives in their work. Reviewing the DVD in conjunction with reading this chapter will be particularly useful to those who are considering using family narratives in their work.

Family support services – The family support providers who participated in this project consistently reported on the power of the narrative approach in providing them a much deeper understanding of the family. One such person, who had been in the field for over 20 years, noted that she had worked with a mother and her infant in the family resource centre for over a year. But until she had conducted the in-depth interviews and written up the family's narrative, she had not been aware that this mother was suffering from postpartum depression. She said she had missed all the cues, which she said she was very familiar with, because she had not paid attention to the mother in this special way.

Another family support provider noted that it was not until she transcribed the interviews and carefully reconstructed the mother's heavily accented words that she realized that she had not fully understood the mother in the past and had been responding to her inappropriately on some occasions.

A typical response to using the narrative was:

This process has been an eye opener for me – I mean many times coming to our play and parenting sessions – but you've never shared this much with me… so it's like I really didn't know a lot about you and your family at all… so… this was a great process for me… so thank you.

Checking in with the family after the interviews were completed and condensed into a narrative allowed the family to emphasize parts of the narrative that held more significance for them. They also deleted or modified information they did not want to include in the narrative. Many families told the family support staff that they finally felt someone actually listened to them. They said they had been asked about various aspects of their lives, for example, about their health status or their child's progress in school, but nobody has listened to their fuller story with such attention before. Some of them found the experience so affirming they wanted to continue with the interviews even when a family crisis, such as the death of an infant, had clearly devastated them. The family support personnel had truly become their source of support. [See DVD: Using Narratives – Families.]

Teachers and administrators in schools – Teachers and administrators in the school system work with families and children from increasingly diverse backgrounds. Meanwhile, they themselves are largely from middle class families of European descent. Enhancing their knowledge about families who are newcomers, live in poverty, or have a child with disabilities will support their efforts to engage with and respond effectively to these families. In documenting the families' narratives, they will be encouraged to reflect on their own beliefs and values and compare them with those of the children and families they serve. They are likely to build more trusting relationships with families whose narratives they have developed, which in turn will help them work together as a team to support the children. They will develop greater appreciation of differences among the children they work with, rather than make assumptions about their cultural or other classifications (Connelly, Phillion & He, 2003). Their educational plans for the children, and the tasks they assign to the children and/or their families, will take into account the families' particular circumstances. As one of our colleagues said, even if you develop only one family's narrative, the experience you gain from that provides a framework for you to think about the many dimensions and complexities of any family you are working with.

Teachers can refer to family narratives they have already developed when they meet with the family to report on the child's progress, or to chart their goals for the next reporting period. If the parents want them to, they can also forward the narrative to the teacher who will work with the child the following year, and/or the principal who may need to make other decisions about the child in partnership with the family.

Teachers and administrators in childcare – In the field of childcare the racial and ethnic diversity of staff has greatly increased in recent years. Although many members of the staff now come from backgrounds that are similar to those of the families they serve, they don't necessarily use their languages, cultures, and common experiences to connect with families in their workplace. In some cases, they may be able to draw upon their own backgrounds and prior experiences to connect with families whose narratives they intend to develop. This work will not only deepen their knowledge of the rich diversity of families they work with, but also affirm the value of their cultural and linguistic heritage in their workplace.

Social workers – Riessman and Quinney (2005) claim that in the field of social work the use of narratives facilitates better communication across racial and class boundaries. Assumptions we make on the basis of our own racial and socio-economic locations are challenged by the fuller, more complex accounts of lives of families we do not interact with on a regular basis in our everyday social lives.

By listening to families' stories, social workers will become more aware of strengths that already exist in a family system. By shifting the focus from deficits to strengths, they will be better equipped to help the family recognize and draw upon their strengths to deal with present or future crises. This can be a transformative experience for some families. Social workers can then help families develop specific strategies that fit their particular features, or find resources that match their particular needs, which can lead to higher levels of functioning (Lietz, 2007).

Family narratives developed by social workers provide records that they can refer to and build upon in their work with the family. They focus on what the family considers important information, which may be missed in standardized forms used in some institutions. They are a useful starting point for keeping track of how each member of the family is doing, and what impact that has on other members of the family. The narrative can also be shared with another case worker if and when needed, again, we emphasize, with the permission of the family.

Health professionals – Ekman and Skott (2005) claim that using narratives in nursing is helpful in understanding patient experience. The clinical knowledge gained by carefully listening to one family can help in the nursing care of other families, too. Narratives have also been used as a therapeutic tool to support terminally ill patients by encouraging them to reminisce and reflect on their lives (Bochner, 2001; Noble & Jones, 2005). Health professionals also find that families experiencing the death or illness of a loved one often find comfort in creating their narratives.

Family doctors in particular can use family narratives in important ways to help families keep healthy, to make accurate diagnosis, and to recommend interventions that will be appropriately used. Because family doctors are often the first professionals to whom families report their concerns about physical or mental illness, they need to have fuller, holistic information about the family. The need for such detailed information is being recognized more widely, as leaders in the medical profession pay more attention to the evidence pointing to the social determinants of health.

Health professionals who work in the area of mental health especially need information about the family as a unit. The reasons for poor mental health are often located in familial relations, and the healing process is also often dependent on familial support. Newcomer families, families living in poverty, or those who have a child with a disability experience a great deal of stress. Mental health professionals need to know their particular circumstances in order to respond to them appropriately.

While family doctors or medical specialists need information about particular families they serve, public health professionals also need, at least in a general way, to understand families' lives holistically in order to address their health issues more effectively. For example, they need to know what information families need, what happens when a family member is ill for a long time, or what prevents children or adults from taking medication they are prescribed. [See DVD: Using Narratives – Professional Practice.]

Professors – College and university professors who prepare professionals to work in any of these or other public services will find that the process of developing narratives will remind them of the complexities, dilemmas, and conundrums of working with families. It will help them resist the temptation to provide generic answers to their students' questions and instead direct their attention to contextual factors that make each problem somewhat unique. This does not mean that they should not teach their students general principles to guide their practice. What it does mean is that they should emphasize that principles need to be interpreted and nuanced according to the particular circumstances of each family, rather than applied as standardized rules.

Listening to families and developing their narratives will help professors experience first hand what it is like to work with families to develop their narratives. They will be better positioned to encourage their students, whether they are teachers, social workers, health professionals, or other service providers, to systematically develop narratives of families they work with. Professors will be better prepared to help their students plan more carefully, listen more deeply, record more accurately, analyze the interviews more thoughtfully, and edit narratives more collaboratively if they have experienced the process personally. They will also be able to point to the challenges and rewards of doing this work if they have done it themselves.

When professors have access to a set of family narratives, they can use them as cases to help their students identify the particular circumstances, strengths, and challenges of each family, and think about how they would respond to that family in their professional roles. The narratives at the end of this book are included for this purpose. While we have attached some questions to these narratives as examples, professors preparing professionals in different fields may want to use different kinds of questions. These questions can easily be created to suit the instructional goals selected by the professor. Alternatively, students could be asked to first read the narratives in their entirety and then to create the questions themselves, which they will most likely do from their own professional perspectives.

Some professors may be able to organize simulated client exercises using professional actors who have taken on the roles of families whose narratives have been documented (see Frankel & Corson, 2003, and DVD: Simulation). This involves inviting students to interview the actors in their roles as family members and provides feedback immediately afterwards. The feedback provided by the professor, as well as by the actors and the peers in the classroom, can be a very powerful learning experience.

Students – The use of family narratives in the classroom can provide students with insights into lives of families who may be very different from their own. It could help them see these families in a more holistic way rather than in their essentialized categories, simply as newcomer parents, or parents of a child with disabilities, for example. The narratives can challenge their prior assumptions, for example, that newcomer families don't know English or French, or that they always live in poverty. They can help them develop empathy and understanding, but also an appreciation for the strengths, resilience, and complexities of families. Reading and responding to family narratives can temper any inclination to see families simply as victims, or as unthinking individuals who resist expert advice. Whether this work is done simply by responding to the written narratives or through simulated client exercises, the opportunity for students to plan and test their responses in a safe environment is invaluable experience in preparing them to work with real families.

Working with narratives in the classroom will enable the students to discuss true to life complex situations which they are likely to encounter in their careers (Frankel & Corson, 2003). They will have the opportunity to practise problem-solving and decision-making skills by identifying and addressing the issues raised by the narrative accounts (Hinyard & Kreuter, 2006) with little risk to themselves or real families they will work with in future.

When students are involved in the development of the narratives they also gain experience in approaching families, listening to them with respectful attention, systematically collecting and documenting their narratives. When students do this work under the supervision of an educator, their questions are answered, their uncertainties addressed, and their work critiqued. This experience will serve them well in their professional practice where close supervision of their early attempts to engage with families may not always be possible. [See DVD: Using Narratives - Education: Pre-Service and In-Service.]

Families – The experience of constructing their narratives can be rewarding for families. Several of the families interviewed in this project commented on feeling affirmed and stronger as a result of their participation. One of the male participants thanked the interviewer with tears in his eyes for documenting his family's narrative so faithfully, and said, "Yes, that's me. That's us. Thank you for doing this for us!"

The families consistently appreciated the opportunity to be "really listened to". They especially valued the interviewers' interest in their full stories rather than in gathering fragmented information about them, such as about their health problems or their financial challenges. The families often welcomed the interviewers into their homes and talked to them at great length. Stronger, more trusting relationships were established with service providers. Several interviewers remarked that they thought families they approached would agree to participate but they were surprised by the enthusiasm with which they were met, particularly after the first session.

The process of developing narratives offered the families an opportunity to identify and reflect upon their values, strengths, priorities, strategies, and challenges. They created coherent stories of their lives as they described the past and present contexts in which their lives were located.

Copies of the final narratives are given to them to use as they wish.

With a clear description of their own history, values, beliefs and aspirations for their child, the families can bring their narrative to other professionals who provide them with services – a doctor, a teacher, a settlement worker. For families who are often relocated to other locations across Canada, such as military families, the narrative provides an introductory segue into the service support system they will encounter. The families are relieved of the burden of retelling the cultural-historical context of their lives to each professional they meet. The richness of the narrative moves beyond typical social checklists and health surveys. Over time, as the families reflect on their narrative, they can update it to include new events and experiences, or modify it to suit new purposes.

Professionals in many fields advocate for listening to families' narratives. However, their practice does not necessarily match this intention because they may feel obligated to offer some intervention. Simply listening to families is difficult for service providers who are trained to respond to them by offering information, advice, or expert opinion. Health professionals, for example, have found that when patients tell their stories they develop a better understanding of their illness, and often find peace, optimism, and greater meaning in their lives (Bochner, 2001; Skott, 2001). In practice, however, only patients who are unlikely to benefit from any medical intervention are the ones who have the privilege of telling their life stories, usually to volunteers and not staff members (Talat, personal communication).

Summary

Families provide the primary context for and have a major influence on the healthy growth and development of their children. Families today take a wide variety of forms. Whether they are headed by two different or same sex parents, a single parent, or in some cases grandparents, families are responsible for nurturing, protecting and guiding their children. Internal factors such as illness within the family or external factors such as legislative requirements can act as supports or barriers to the family's successful functioning.

Service providers in education, child care, early intervention, family support, health, and social welfare work in publicly funded institutions whose mandate is to support families to take care of their children. Service providers such as these may find it difficult to provide services that take into account the diverse values, needs, and interests of children and families, particularly those who are usually marginalized in Canadian society. The project *Listening to Families: Reframing Services* was designed to increase the capacity of service providers to engage with families who are newcomers, live in poverty, or have a child with a disability of some kind, using family narrative as a way to get to know the family. This can be an effective tool for building trust and synergy with families who might otherwise not have their voices heard. Our hope is that service provisions in Canada will be shaped and changed by families' narratives, and Canadian families' narratives will change as better services ensure the wellbeing of the family and their children.

In using the family narrative approach, service providers must embrace a paradigm that may be new to some of them. The narrative interviews are not designed to determine the family's needs, deficits, or dysfunction, but rather to hear the voice of the family. What is the family's perspective on having a child with a disability? What is the newcomer family's dream for their children? What strategies has a family already tried to move towards their goals? What supports can the service provider use to assist the family in reaching their goal?

The family narrative approach views the family as having unique values and strengths. It shifts the locus of control to the family to use its own resources and strategies, access others with the support of service providers, and formulate new service possibilities.

The service provider as an effective listener must resist the urge to advise, analyze or judge behaviour. The families' strengths, beliefs, and aspirations become the centrepiece from which new service options are designed and old ones adapted. Rather than determining in which program or intervention offered by a service agency the family will fit, the agency develops services to fit the needs of the family.

The Future of the Listening to Families Approach

The use of the family narrative approach holds great promise for service providers in family support programs, education, early intervention, child care, health, social welfare and related professions. Although feedback from those who have developed family narratives has been extraordinarily positive, we are still left with questions such as:

> Can service providers maintain use of the narrative approach over the long term?
> In what ways can family narratives influence service provision itself?
> What is the long-term effect on families of telling the narrative?
> What are the practical and ethical implications of sharing information about families within an institution?
> While we, and many of our collaborators, we hope, will continue to explore these questions, we also hope you will try to develop the narratives of some families you work with and share what you learn in the process with us.

References

Abbot, D.A, & Meredith, W.H. (1986). Strengths of parents with retarded children. *Family Relations, 35,* 371-375.

Ali, M. (2008). Loss of parenting self-efficacy among immigrant parents, *Contemporary Issues in Early Childhood,* 9(2), pg. 148-160.

Ali, M., & Kilbride, K. M. (2004). *Forging New Ties: Improving parenting and family support services for new Canadians with young children.* Ottawa: Human Resources and Skills Development Canada.

Aycan, Z. & Kanungo, R.N. (1998). Impact of acculturation on socialization beliefs and behaviour occurrences among Indo-Canadian immigrants. *Journal of Comparative Family Studies,* 29(3), 451-468.

Beckman, P.J., Newcomb, S., Frank, N., and Brown, L. (1996). Evolution of working relationships with families. In P.J. Beckman (Ed.), *Strategies for Working with Families of Young Children with Disabilities.* Baltimore: Brookes. pp. 17-30.

Beiser, M., Hou, F., Hyman, I. & Tousignant, M. (2002). Poverty, family process, and the mental health of immigrant children in Canada. *American Journal of Public Health,* 92(2), 220-227.

Bochner, A. P. (2001). Narrative's virtues. *Qualitative Inquiry, 7(2),* 131-157.

Bronfenbrenner, U. (1979). *The Ecology of Human Development: Experiments by nature and design.* Cambridge, MA: Harvard University Press.

Bronfenbrenner, U. (1986). Ecology of the Family as a Context for Human Development: research perspectives, *Developmental Psychology,* 22(6), 723-742. http://dx.doi.org/10.1037/0012-1649.22.6.723

Campaign 2000 "Factsheets: Defining Poverty". November, 2003. Toronto: Campaign 2000. Retrieved June 27, 2007.http://www.campaign2000.ca/res/fs/FS_DefiningPoverty.pdf

Canadian Association for Community Living, (2008). 2008 National Report Card: Inclusion of Canadians with Intellectual Disabilities. Retrieved from http://www.cacl.ca/english/documents/ReportCards/2008ReportCard_Nov 26.pdf April 16, 2009.

Clandinin, J. (2007). *Handbook of Narrative Inquiry: Mapping a methodology.* London: Sage.

Conle, C. (2003). An anatomy of narrative curricula. *Educational Researcher,* 32(3), 3-15.

Connelly, F.M. & Clandinin, D.J. (1988). *Teachers as Curriculum Planner: Narratives of experience.* Toronto, ON: OISE Press.

Connelly, F.M., Phillion, J., & He, M.F. (2003). An exploration of narrative inquiry into multiculturalism in education: Reflecting on two decades of research in an inner-city Canadian community school. *Curriculum Inquiry,* 33(4), pg. 363-384.

DeYoung, A.J. (1994). Children at risk in America's rural schools: Economic and cultural dimensions. In R. J. Rossi (Ed.), *Schools and Students at Risk: Context and framework for positive change* (pp. 229–251). New York: Teachers College Press.

Dunst, C.J., Trivette, C.M., Davis, M. & Cornwell, J. (1988). Enabling and empowering families of children with health impairments. *Children's Health Care,* 17(2), pg. 71-81.

Eggenberger, S.K. & Nelms, T.P. (2007). Family interviews as a method for family research. *Journal of Advanced Nursing,* 58(3), 282-292.

Ekman, I. & Skott, C. (2005). Developing clinical knowledge through a narrative-based method of interpretation. *European Journal of Cardiovascular Nursing, 4(3),* 251-256.

Evans, P. (1995). Children and youth at risk. In Organisation for Economic Cooperation and Development, *Our Children at Risk.* Paris: Organisation for Economic Cooperation and Development, pp. 13-50.

Evans, P., & Hurrell, P. (1996). Introduction. In Organisation for Economic Cooperation and Development Centre for Education Research and Innovation, *Successful Services for our Children and Families at Risk* (pp. 19–37). Paris: Organisation for Economic Co-operation and Development.

Fiese, B.H. & Spagnola, M. (2005). Narratives in and about families: An examination of coding schemes and a guide for family researchers. *Journal of Family Psychology,* 19, 51-61.

Frankel, E.B. (2004). Supporting inclusive care and education for young children with special needs and their families: An international perspective. *Childhood Education.* Retrieved July 11, 2007 http://findarticles.com/p/articles/mi_qa3614/is_200401/ai_n9376423

Garcia-Coll, C. & Szalacha, L.A. (2004). The multiple contexts of middle childhood, *The Future of Children,* 14(2), 81-97. http://dx.doi.org/10.2307/1602795

Garcia-Coll, C., Lambert, G., Jenkins, R., McAdoo, H.P., Crnic, K., Wasik, B.H. & Vazquez Garcia, H.A. (1996). An integrative model for the study of the developmental competencies in minority children, *Child Development* 67(5), 1891-1914. http://dx.doi.org/10.2307/1131600

Gordon, V. & Nocon, H. (2008) Reproducing segregation: Parent involvement, diversity and school governance. *Journal of Latinos and Education* 7 (4) 320-339

Harris, A. & Goodall, J. (2008) Do parents know they matter? Engaging all parents in learning. *Educational Researcher* 50 (3) 277-289.

Heath, H. (2006). Parenting: A relationship oriented and competency based process. *Child Welfare,* 85(5), 749-766.

Hendry, P.H. (2007). The future of narrative. *Qualitative Inquiry,* 12(4), 487-499.

Hertzman, C. (2002). *Leave no child behind! Social exclusion and child development.* Toronto. The Laidlaw Foundation.

Hinyard, Leslie, J. & Kreuter, M. W. (2007). Using narrative communication as a tool for health behavior change: A conceptual, theoretical, and empirical overview. *Health Education and & Behaviour, 34(5),* 777-792.

Holden, G.W. & Hawk, C. (2003). Meta-parenting in the journey of child-rearing: A mechanism for change, in L. Kuczinsky (Ed.) *Handbook of Dynamics in Parent-Child Relations,* pp 189-210. Thousand Oaks, CA: Sage Publications.

Irwin, S.H., Lero, D.S., & Brophy, K. (2000). A matter of urgency: Including children with special needs in child care in Canada. Wreck Cove, NS: Breton Books.

Irwin, S.H., & Lero, D.S. (2004). In our way: Child care barriers to full workforce participation experienced by parents of children with special needs – and potential remedies. Retrieved from http://www.specialinkcanada.org/books/iow_summary.html. July 9, 2008.

Irwin, S. H., Lero, D. S., & Brophy, K. (2004). Inclusion: The next generation in child care in Canada (pp. 265-267). Wreck Cove, N.S.: Breton Books

Kerr, D. & Beaujot, R. (2003). Child poverty and family structure in Canada, 1981-1997. *Journal of Comparative Family Studies.* 34,3; 321-335.

Krames, J.A. (2002). *The Rumsfeld Way: Leadership wisdom of a battle-hardened maverick.* NY: McGraw-Hill.

Kuntz, S. and Hesslar, A. (1998): Bridging the gap between theory and practice: Fostering active learning through the case method. Paper presented at the Annual Meeting of the Association of American Colleges and Universities (AAC&U): 23.

Lai, Y., & Ishiyama, F.I. (2004). Involvement of immigrant Chinese Canadian mothers of children with disabilities. *Exceptional Children, 71,* 97-108.

Lessenberry, B.M., & Rehfeldt, R.A. (2004). Evaluating stress levels of parents of children with disabilities. *Exceptional Children, 70,* 231-244.

Levin, B. (1995). Educational responses to poverty. *Canadian Journal of Education.* 20(3), 211-224.

Li, P. (1998) The market value and social value of race, in V. Satzewich (Ed). *Racism and Social Inequality in Canada,* 115-130. Toronto: Thompson Educational.

Li, P. (2003) Initial earnings and catch-up capacity of immigrants, *Canadian Public Policy,* 29(3), 319-337. http://dx.doi.org/10.2307/3552289

Liamputtong, P. (2001). Motherhood and the challenge of immigrant mothers: A personal reflection. *Families in Society, 82*(2), 195-201.

Lietz, C. (2007). Uncovering stories of family resilience: A mixed methods study of resilient families, Part 2. *Journal of Contemporary Social Services,* 88(1), 147-155.

MacNaughton, G. (2005). *Doing Foucault in early childhood studies: Applying poststructural ideas.* New York: Routledge.

McKeown, J. Clarke, A. and Repper, J. (2007). Life story work in health and social care: Systematic literature review. *Journal of Advanced Nursing,* 55(2), 237-247.

Noble, A. & Jones, C. (2005). Benefits of narrative therapy: Holistic interventions at the end of life, *British Journal of Nursing,* 14(6), 330-333.

Noddings, N. (2005). Identifying and responding to needs in education, *Cambridge Journal of Education,* 35(2), 147-159. http://dx.doi.org/10.1080/03057640500146757

Odom, S.L. (2000). Preschool inclusion: What we know and where we go from here. *Topics in Early Childhood Special Education, 20,* 20-28.

Razack, S. (1998). *Looking White People in the Eye: Race, gender and culture in courtrooms and classrooms.* Toronto: University of Toronto Press.

Reissman, C.K., & Quinney, L. (2005). Narrative in social work: A Critical Review. *Qualitative Social Work. 4(4),* pp. 391-412.

Reitz, J. G. (2001) Immigrant success and changing national institutions: Recent trends in Canada, a U.S. comparison, and policy options. Paper presented at Re-inventing Society in a Changing Global Economy Conference, Toronto, 8-10 March.

Reitz, J. G. & Banerjee, R. (2007). *Racial Inequality, Social Cohesion, and Policy Issues in Canada.* Montreal: Institute for Research on Public Policy.

Roer-Strier, D. (2001) Reducing risk for children in changing cultural contexts: Recommendations for intervention and training, *Child Abuse and Neglect,* 25, 231-248.

Rossiter, M. (1999). A narrative approach to development: Implications for adult education. *Adult Education Quarterly,* 50(1), pg. 56-71.

Rothman, Laurel. (2007). Oh Canada! Too many children in poverty for too long. *Education Canada.* 47, 4; 49-53.

Royal Commission on Aboriginal Peoples, 1996. Volume 1 - Looking Forward Looking Back, Part Two: False Assumptions and a Failed Relationship, Chapter 10 - Residential Schools-Discipline and Abuse. Indian and Northern Affairs, Canada
http://www.ainc-inac.gc.ca/ch/rcap/sg/sg31_e.html#104

Schissel, B. and Wotherspoon, T. (2001). The business of placing Canadian children and youth "at-risk". *Canadian Journal of Education.* 26(3).

Schorr, L. (1988). *Within Our Reach: Breaking the cycle of disadvantage.* New York: DoubleDay.

Scott, R., Sexton, D., & Wood, T. (1986). *A comparison of marital adjustment and stress of parents of typical and atypical infants.* Paper presented at the meeting of the International Council for Exceptional Children Conference, New Orleans, LA.

Seat, R. (2003). Factors affecting the settlement and adaptation process of Canadian adolescent newcomers 16-19 years of age, in P. Anisef & K.M. Kilbride (Eds) *Managing Two Worlds: The experiences and concerns of immigrant youth in Ontario.* Toronto: Canadian Scholars' Press.

Skott, C. (2001). Caring narratives and the strategy of presence: Narrative communication in nursing practice and research. *Nursing Science Quarterly,* 14, 249-254.

Squire, C. (2005). Reading narratives. *Group Analysis, 38(1),* 91-107.

Tannen, Deborah. (1990). *You just don't understand: Women and men in conversation.* New York: William Morrow.

Trivette, C.M. & Dunst C.J. (2005). Community-based parent support programs In Tremblay, R.E., Barr, R.G., Peters, R.DeV., eds. *Encyclopaedia on Early Childhood Development* [online]. Montreal, Quebec: Centre of Excellence for Early Childhood Development, 1-8. Available at http://www.childencyclopedia.com/documents/Trivette-DunstANGxp.pdf.

Trute, B., and Hiebert-Murphy, D. (2007). The implications of "Working Alliance" for the measurement and evaluation of family-centered practice in childhood disability services. *Infants and Young Children,* 20(2), 109-119.

Turnbull, A.P., Turbiville, V., & Turnbull, H.R. (2000). Evolution of family-professional partnerships: Collective empowerment as the model for the early twenty-first century. In J.P. Shonkoff & S.J. Meisels (Eds.), *Handbook of early childhood intervention* (2nd ed) (pp.630-650). Cambridge:

Cambridge University Press.

Turney, K. & Kao, G. (2009) Barriers to school involvement: Are immigrant parents disadvantaged? *The Journal of Educational Research* 102 (4) 257-271

Vajda, J. (2007). Two survivor cases: Therapeutic effect as side product of the biographical narrative interview. *Journal of Social Work Practice,* 21(1), 89-102.

Xu, Y. (2007). Empowering culturally diverse families of young children with disabilities: The double ABCX model. *Early Childhood Education Journal, 34,* 431-437.

The Cressy Family

A family with children with disabilities

April was twenty-one when she had her twin boys Johnny and Jake, now thirteen, and moved out of her parents' home. With the help of Capital Region Housing she found a condo. She was on welfare one month before she had her boys. Although she and Joe, the father of the twins, were together during the first few months of their sons' lives, they separated shortly after. For the next twelve years she was a single mother, with the occasional live-in boyfriend. Currently, April lives in a condo she rents from her parents, with her sons and her boyfriend of a year and a half, Rick, and their daughter Nicole, now seven months old. April and Joe have worked out an arrangement in which the boys spend every second weekend and alternate holidays with him.

Early on in her boy's life April had concerns about the twins' abilities. She felt that they just "did not act like normal infants". She noticed obvious speech delays; Johnny started crawling very late and Jack just swam across the floor. April was quick to consult professionals; as a parent she had a feeling that something was wrong, and determined to figure out what was going on. She enrolled them in Early Head Start, where they were given the Developmental Inventory for Screening Children (the DISC assessment). She was relieved to find a service provider who was open to listen to her concerns. "They found that they were severely delayed in eight major developmental areas". Once she had a diagnosis, she continued to work hard for the necessary supports for her boys.

Most of the boys' supports have been found in the educational setting. April enrolled them for three years in an Early Education program, which allowed for smaller classrooms, teaching through play and speech therapy. At the end, they were diagnosed again and found to have cognitive delays and behavioral issues. They were accepted into the Opportunity Fund program at an elementary school, where they found themselves in a classroom with children of varying abilities, from mild cognitive delays to autism. In this setting April unfortunately noticed a lot of behavioral issues. Quite often April, and later Rick, was being called to come and pick up the boys, Johnny especially, for his behavior, which often included fighting. Early on, even if the teachers were not labeling the students, the twins started to apply the labels of "challenged" and "gifted." At times April saw her boys using the fact that they were too 'stupid' to attempt a new activity or challenge. April and Rick began hearing the boys say, "Oh well, I am stupid; I can't do that."

April recognized the boys' need for support, so she confronted the labeling of her children head on and worked with their teachers. This past year the boys moved to high school, which offered a much needed new outlook on working with the boys' challenges. April noticed the teachers'

knowledge, commitment, and compassion for the children they were working with. She felt "They are not only trained in how to deal with children with behavioral issues…but they actually like what they do." The program, based on positive affirmation, exemplified the type of educational support the boys needed. The boys were both in their own classes, able to build identities of their own. The number of suspension phone calls decreased to none at all.

"Through the schools I have had… lots of support, but at the same time …a large part of it was because I was very active". At home, April tried to maintain a constant, stable environment, as the boys suffer from too much change. She emphasized the importance of consistency to her parents and especially to Joe, who are all partners in supporting the boys' development. Joe is learning how to deal with some of their struggles. When he speaks to the boys and gives them simple instructions, and they do not follow through properly, he easily gets frustrated and confused, not remembering they need detailed instructions and to be supported through them.

April makes great efforts in supporting her children at home, and finding support for them. She accepts them for who they are, and for the abilities they have. April hopes her support for her boys' abilities and their strengths, as well as her hopes and dreams for their future, instils confidence and self awareness in them, which is something April herself did not receive in her youth, and has struggled with in her adulthood. The reality of her struggles with low self esteem and low self respect came to a head when she was offered crack cocaine by a boyfriend at the time. She was familiar with using substances in order to escape some of her harsh realities. When she tried cocaine, she had found the perfect escape: April agreed with a friend who said, "It took me twenty years to become an alcoholic …[and] twenty minutes to become a crack addict".

April's boys were six at the time that she stared using cocaine, and April did her best to shelter them from her addiction, which lead to her leading somewhat of a double life. For the longest time, she was able to lead this life, but the consequences of her actions started to become increasingly evident. She wouldn't have her rent money or enough money for food, and in general, she just didn't care. Her life continued spiralling out of control until she was confronted with the consequences of her actions directly. She was sitting at table, with a bunch of crack addicts and she was asking them how she could keep her kids from starting cocaine, as she was reaching for the pipe. Even though she was high at the time, she was able to realize the best way to discourage her children from doing drugs would logically be not to do them herself.

Now that she had recognized the issue, the many steps to follow were time consuming, and personally challenging. For the most part she was on her own, and her steps faltered when went back to her addiction. Although initially she felt like the reason she wanted to get clean was for her children, she quickly realized that it needed to be first and foremost for herself. She joined an online support group and enrolled in the NA twelve-step program, doing 90 meetings in 90 days, where she learnt the premise of what she needed to do.

After six months of being clean, April started to give back to the programs that offered her such support. On Christmas Eve she ran a de-tox meeting where she met Rick, the boyfriend who one year later fathered Nicole. Today, April has been clean for a year and a half and has continued her service within NA as a Public Information volunteer. She feels "one of the best ways to stay in recovery is to stay in the middle." Even to this day her boys are not sure to what extent their mother had entered into the drug world.

April and Rick have high hopes for their new family. They work hard to keep consistent activities in their household. For example, every Friday they have a family game night. Also, April and Rick are working hard to instil the importance of reading in the kids, so every night they make a point of reading a story to everyone. The experience of being a father has changed Joe immensely, "even though other people cannot see it, it has made [him] want to become more of a man." April is very optimistic, as well as realistic for her boys' future. She could certainly see them going to some sort of technical college like Northern Alberta Institute of Technology (NAIT) or Grant MacEwan, while Rick feels that "they could be Prime Minister if they wanted to be". For April, hearing from her thirteen-year-old son that the "one thing that he will do that she never did was not drink, do drugs, or smoke" was one of her proudest moments as a parent. "I'm sorry that you …can't see it. But things have changed huge in my life. But a lot of the changes come from inside before you're going to see them on the outside. If there is anything that I would say to other families, [it] is to humble yourselves enough to ask for help when you need it."

Discussion Questions:

> What strengths do members of this family display? What challenges does this family still face?

> Describe the conditions which have influenced the childrearing techniques of the Cressy family.

> How can service providers support this mother as she struggles to transform the family dynamics through her own insights, growth and success?

The Graffa Family

A family with a child with a disability

Thomas was born into the G. family prematurely, at 3 lbs, 15 oz. His mother, Maria, says, "The first few days I was really afraid. Then the doctor came into my room and started talking about his heart: he had a murmur. That's when he started talking about chromosome 21; I didn't know what chromosome 21 was." Maria spent the next two days crying, thinking about the impact, the responsibilities, and the long-term challenges of raising a son with Down Syndrome. Tony and Maria were offered counselling, and social services set in place a process of support for them.

The first two months were just as hard as the first two days. Maria was adamant about breastfeeding Thomas, but despite expert help and advice, Thomas did not seem able to latch on. Maria's days and nights were spent pumping breast milk, feeding her newborn, changing diapers, making doctor's visits, and trying to deal with the new reality of her life. The one advantage of giving Thomas a bottle was the opportunity it gave Tony to bond with his son.

The tide turned when Maria consulted a naturopath, who massaged Thomas's mouth and stimulated his sucking reflex: Thomas began to breastfeed. Life became much easier for Maria, and good luck seemed to be on her side where Thomas was concerned. She was referred to a community organization in her neighbourhood, who sent in a special educator weekly to work with Thomas. Through this organization, Maria also had the opportunity to meet with other mothers who had children with special needs, to chat and exchange information. One of these mothers has become more than just an acquaintance; Maria is sure they will remain friends as they share the joys and challenges of raising children with Down Syndrome.

Within a surprisingly short time, a wonderful social worker was assigned to the family to provide counselling and help them obtain the resources they needed. Through her networking, Maria found her waiting time at the local re-adaptation centre reduced, and could participate in a weekly Moms and Tots playgroup for families with infants with special needs run by a special educator. Networking also allowed Maria to become a member of the Down Syndrome Association. It has provided her with pertinent information, the opportunity to attend workshops, and recently, two free sessions with a speech pathologist. The wait for services at the Montreal Children's Hospital was short, and once a month Thomas is seen by both a physical and an occupational therapist.

Thomas is now eight months old. Does Maria feel disadvantaged because she has a child with special needs? Quite the contrary. With the professional help and guidance she has received, Maria feels she has acquired a good understanding of child development; she has learned many tricks to stimulate learning; and most importantly, she has gained self-confidence in her abilities as a mother. "It makes me feel I have this knowledge I

want to share with people; and you know, it makes me feel good!"

A few years ago, Maria had become tired of paying rent, and decided they should buy a house. Tony was reluctant at first, but soon became excited when they found their dream home. Although they had been experiencing some difficulties with their marriage, buying the house seems to have been a positive catalyst. At the same time, as she advanced into her thirties, it became important for her to have a child, but it took several years for her to convince Tony that they should have a baby. When Thomas was then diagnosed with Down Syndrome, the guilt and frustration in their daily challenges became enormous, even while the joy and love were also overwhelming. It was clear to Maria, however, that Tony was in denial for a long time; she thinks he saw his abilities and this allowed him to forget about his challenges. Tony is a musician and he shared his love of music with his son. It was exciting to see the joyous response in Thomas when they played at the keyboard together, and Thomas developed new skills; she wondered if Thomas had inherited his father's musical abilities.

But appointments with medical professionals and special educators all seemed to emphasize the reality of Thomas's difficulties. "Then Tony started working at La Senza, and La Senza has a program for adults with disabilities; he sees them one on one, every day. He had a very hard time at the beginning [thinking of Thomas in such a way] so I told him, 'This is why we're doing the stimulation now.'...I think the Thomas issue made us come to terms with the fact that we're not in the same frame."

While Tony and Maria had had some problems as a couple before Thomas was born, they were able to manage. But dealing with the responsibilities of raising a child with special needs emphasized the differences in their attitudes. Maria is a determined woman: when something is important to her, she will take the steps to make it happen. She feels that Thomas needs stability and routine in his life, but Tony likes to live his life in a more unplanned, light-hearted way. Tony's passion for music is time consuming, leaving much of the family responsibility on Maria's shoulders. Maria made the difficult decision to split up with her husband, and they have recently started seeing a mediator. "We both have the interest of making sure Thomas is okay. We want [life] to be as normal as possible for him. Although we're apart, we still want to do things with him as a family, even though we're not."

Life as a single mom is lonely in the evening and scary at times. Maria is confident that things will work out, and she is ready to take on her new life one day at a time. Her family is a constant, positive presence; she has discovered wonderful neighbours, made new friends, found competent medical and educational support, and amazing inner strength.

"It doesn't take much to get Thomas to smile, and that gives me joy. It makes me see things differently. Little things don't bother me anymore. I don't have cancer, his heart is good.... Even with his disability, he has made me see life differently. And life is too short. So that helps carry me through the difficult moments. It's given me the strength to make the decision I did with us as a couple". Maria is optimistic that she has the tools to make her life with Thomas fulfilling and successful.

Discussion Questions:

> Describe how the birth of a child with special needs increased the stress in this family's life.

> How can service providers include the father in the planning and decision-making for Thomas?

> How can this narrative assist you in your professional role to reframe services for this family?

The Hunt Family

A family with a child with disabilities

Carol Hunt is an only child who was born and raised by her mother and grandparents, in a tiny rural community located on the east coast of Newfoundland and Labrador. She has a wonderful relationship with her mother and described her as "a friend, a sister, she's everything in one...even a father." Carol had a happy childhood and benefited from being raised among her mother's siblings. She indicated that she was raised well and all her needs were met adequately. "I had some of ...[what] other children never had......love is the most important thing I ever got from my family." Growing up, she knew who her father was, and his whereabouts, but she did not make any contact with him until approximately six years ago. Carol and her children now have a good relationship with her father.

Carol met her husband, Peter, while attending high school. She left school early to travel to the "mainland" to be with him; here she found employment. However, she returned back to her hometown and obtained her high school diploma before returning to Ontario. Her son Bobby was born in Ontario, but when he was six years old they returned to Peter's hometown. She also has a daughter, Cassy, who is four years old and will be entering kindergarten this coming September.

Carol describes Bobby, now eleven years old, as "a child [who] always wants to be on the go." Bobby was diagnosed with Attention Deficit Disorder (ADD) approximately one year ago and is currently being tested for having "blank out seizures," which Carol described as a condition where, "your brain could stop for 5-10 seconds and then he [must] rethink what he's at and that could put him [in some] emotional [distress]...." Bobby requires a lot of attention, especially from his mother, and suffers from intense mood swings. He is very active and has a hard time focusing on homework or personal tasks. Bobby gets easily angered, to the point where Carol fears the anger may result in his hurting someone or himself. He often becomes frustrated and suffers from episodes where he may not remember his acting out behaviours. When he lashes out at his peers or family members, he can become very upset and angry with himself afterwards. Because of this, Bobby sometimes claims to feel unloved and misunderstood in the family. Carol finds this disheartening because, "he's loved all the time and that hurts. To me, love and comfort [are] everything you can give your child...." Although not entirely comfortable with it, Carol has tried administering medication to Bobby upon the recommendation of professionals. However, she stopped giving it to him because he suffered from side effects, such as intense headaches.

Bobby's condition greatly affects his school performance. He is not integrated into a regular classroom, but has a working space alone where he is taught mostly by a student assistant for a majority of the school day.

This is something that bothers Bobby as he feels isolated from the other children and his peers treat him differently. He has been suspended from traveling to school on the bus for long periods of time as a result of inappropriate behaviour during commuting. Carol believes that sometimes children provoke him because they know he has a short fuse and will get into trouble. Carol felt that his teachers do not understand the reasons for his actions, or how difficult it is for him to control them. She believed that Bobby would perform much better at school if he was given rewards for his efforts. He is rarely permitted to attend school trips or participate in extracurricular activities as punishment for improper behaviour. She felt that the school is working against Bobby instead of trying to find solutions to help him manage his condition. In terms of homework, it takes a great deal of energy and patience to help him complete tasks at home, as it is so difficult for him to focus. When it comes to testing, Carol claimed that if Bobby could answer test questions verbally instead of having to write them on paper he would get much better marks.

Carol feels the affects of Bobby's condition. She works long hours at the local fish plant and is exhausted by the end of her shifts. Her husband usually works away from home, and has been absent for up to seven months at a time. Although this is very hard on Carol, she still feels supported by Peter through nightly phone calls and visits home whenever possible. Her children are cared for by a grandparent or other family members when she is working. Carol said one of the biggest challenges of having a child with ADD is that, "people don't know what he's going through." She finds it hard when other adults stop and stare or pass judgment. Often times, she has had to bring him inside the house when playing outside with other children "because he's angry, he's upset, he's crying, he's screeching, he's throwing rocks, and hating himself and the world and thinking he's nothing." Fortunately, Carol does have close friends who are supportive and understand the challenges she faces. She attends Bingo at the local hall whenever she has the chance, but admits it is very difficult to find any time for herself; "even using the bathroom by myself is a pleasure." Carol and Peter rarely spend any time together, but there are times they will find a babysitter and go to the family cabin for a night alone.

Carol is very thankful for the local Family Resource Center (FRC). She has taken part in various parenting programs, and especially enjoyed networking with others. "You always think it's only you going through it, but there's more than you out there. And when you get to know that, there's a big relief off you." Carol continues to attend programs at the FRC and she has a great relationship with the staff members there, where she knows she can get the support she needs. Currently, the town offers very little for children outside of the school. There are no recreational activities or organized groups where children like Bobby can channel their energy. Carol believed that if there were more structured programs in the community, or a place where Bobby could go, his time outside the school and home would be spent more productively. She worries about him when he leaves the house and worries that his condition and behaviour might cause him or others harm. In addition, there are no support groups in the area for parents with children who have ADD or any other kind of special need. Carol has also lost all her trust in our health system ever since social workers showed up unannounced at her door because of a report that Bobby was being abused in the home. The incident has traumatized Carol, as she believed they were going to remove Bobby from her care that day. After questioning Bobby and the family, the social workers concluded the report contained no merit and saw no reason or cause for concern in the home. However, it has shaken Carol's belief in the people around her and in the school system, as she does not know where the report originated. Bobby was also shaken up by the event in his home; he felt hurt, scared, and confused.

Carol does her best to provide a good home for her children and takes things one day at a time. She faces challenges head on and tries to keep a positive attitude. She wishes Bobby did not have this condition, but admits that is has made her a stronger person. "He's making me stronger, and his love....Bobby's love is stronger than mine sometimes." She hopes that one day she will be able to help other parents who are facing similar situations by sharing her story. Her wish for her children is that they grow into strong, loving, and caring adults. When asked what qualities she would like for Bobby to have, her answer comes easily, "Love. And family is everything. And love each other." When asked to share her proudest moment as a parent she said, "Every moment. I can't just pick out one because every moment is precious."

Discussion Questions:

> What are the strengths in this family's narrative? What are the stressors?
> How can services providers collaborate with the family to overcome challenges they face?
> What steps would you take to include Bobby on a collaborative team to develop his individual learning strategies?

The Larson Family

A family with a child with disabilities

Candice Larson lives in western Canada with her father, husband, and three daughters aged thirteen, eleven, and eight. After fifteen years of living in the United States, the Larson family moved back home. Candice teaches nursing at a community college and her husband, Mike, is a salesman for an established company. They both work full time. She likes to go to her mosque regularly, but as she stated, "It is for [my] children." Her first two children are very typical children, but the youngest one, Riel, is a child with significant developmental delays.

Riel is a "happy girl, she doesn't feel her disadvantages." She has developmental delays, visual impairments, and speech impairments. She has speech therapy regularly and educational supports to improve her cognitive functioning. She used to have physiotherapy (PT) and occupational therapy (OT), but that is now completed.

After two healthy pregnancies and two healthy children, Candice was not prepared to deal with a child with special needs. Candice said, "It is just devastating for the family and you just grasp at the roots, and you just say, this is what we are faced with, and you move on." Candice is worried about her oldest daughter, because she puts a lot of responsibility on her in terms of babysitting and helping out. As a family they are trying very hard. Sometimes it is very frustrating. "It [the disability] takes away a lot of what you would typically do as a family." Even if Candice could, she wouldn't change a single thing about Riel.

"Having Riel around … taught us to lessen the arrogance a little bit, come down to earth. We learned a lot from her: she has taught us patience, she has taught us unity for sure, how to work together as a family, she taught us tolerance."

While the Larson family lived in the United States, they had to pay for medical services and all the recreational activities for Riel. It was a big surprise and a relief to find out that "Canada has a tremendous support system," which Candice is very satisfied with. Candice said, "When Riel was just three and four years old, people were coming to the house giving …therapy…." All the activities and services were very affordable for them, and most of it was free. Since Candice was "tapping into a public system", getting services for Riel, like speech and occupational therapy and physiotherapy, she found out about a volunteer system that supported Riel in activities like swimming and gymnastics at the local recreational centre. Later she found out about Supported Childcare and an Infant Development Program (IDP) playgroup. Candice was taking her daughter there on a regular basis, at least once a week. At the playgroup she met other parents and met them at family picnics, "It's all about networking…It is brilliant, brilliant." Candice receives a lot of information

from authorities in her province. However, she feels that there is not enough information for parents regarding where to go for help and how to find all these services. Candice says, "There is nothing saying …we can help you, come, call us, if you have questions. How can agencies make themselves more known?" Candice wishes that her own doctor would have been more proactive. The only thing Candice regrets is that she did not follow up with a phone call to IDP; as a result, she feels that she wasted 6 months when her daughter was just one year old.

At school, Riel has an Individual Education Plan (IEP) and she has one-on-one help in the classroom. "She follows same curriculum, but it is modified to suit her needs." Riel follows the rules of the classroom and meets the standards, but "anything academic, she has not met."

Today Riel is leaving the public schools system, where they have helped her in the past three years because Candice has found out about Mediated Learning Academy. Candice says: " I was not dissatisfied, I loved the public school system, but this school will better serve her needs."

Over the years Candice's expectations and goals have changed for Riel. She continues to support Riel's growth and development through various learning activities and to foster her independence. Candice hopes that Riel will be "self sustained, so she is able to take care of herself and she is able to hold her job, and she is able to be a contributing member of this society. That's what I want for her."

Discussion Questions:

> What is the impact of a child with a disability on the family dynamics in the Larson family?

> How can a service provider collaborate with Carmen's siblings to support them in their lives?

> Describe approaches which service providers can use to assist the mother in meeting the goals she has set for Carmen.

The Miller Family

A family with a child with disabilities

Bob is a stay-at-home dad who works part time delivering local newspapers. His wife works full time for the municipality. After they were married they moved from a large urban centre to the small city in which they currently live. At forty-two years of age, Bob is a little younger than his wife. They have three boys: Luke is seven years old, Mark is five, and the youngest, Owen, is two. According to Bob, the boys are like any other typical children who love to do anything that is physically active. The enjoy playing with blocks and trucks and are huge fans of Batman. They also enjoy puzzles and listening to mom and dad read them books. Luke, the oldest, is described as "outgoing, fun-loving, and personable"

At the age of three, Luke was diagnosed with Duchene Muscular Dystrophy. Bob states the reason Luke was not diagnosed earlier was, "probably due to me; I was in denial, because he wasn't walking or talking fast enough and I was just saying it's because all kids are different." Duchene Muscular Dystrophy, Bob explained is "a degenerative muscle disease... it's the wasting of the muscles....it usually starts in the thighs and calves." The disease is progressive. "Eventually they need a walker or they get to a wheelchair and then in a wheelchair their lungs weaken and death usually occurs between....worse case scenario seventeen [and] ... best case scenario forty-four;... it comes down to the patient." Bob also specifies Duchene Muscular Dystrophy is rare and that only two percent of Duchene patients are affected cognitively. Bob characterizes his seven-year-old son as "acting like a three- to four-year old child socially and emotionally." He hugs, clings, and grabs children often. He is just now learning how to use the toilet. Bob says that although Luke is outgoing, at times he is shy; and he is intelligent enough to know when he's being ostracized by his peers.

Since Bob is the primary caregiver, he spends his morning getting the children ready for school, taking them on walks to the park, the local mall, the pawn shop, or just on their cul-de-sac playing and drawing with chalk on the road. Through the years, Bob and his family have used various programs and agencies which Bob believes are "interconnected". They have visited the local Ontario Early Years Centre near their house where they played in the drop-in and also participated in parenting programs. He felt his experience at that site was a good one: "Luke fit in nicely…. It was really great…really, really good."

As a couple, both Bob and Mary have attended couple's counseling and have taken parenting classes. Bob has also participated in a local dad's parenting class. "I didn't come in here as a bad parent. I came in here because a friend in the 'Fathers make a Difference Program' told me it was a good program…and I learned from the program…that I can improve being a father… I talk more to my children…like eye to eye…" He hasn't visited any of the other local Ontario

Early Years Centres and the reason he has cited for that is "I'm a guy and I've been doing this for seven years now. I've learned there are a lot of women in this situation and very few men and the guys are always in transition. They're just doing it for now… As a man in… a traditional woman's field, it's hard to make friends. And when I do make friends, because of the neighbourhood… there is a lot of turnover." Bob and Mary have also enrolled their children in municipal activities such as swimming and playgroups. They have had positive experiences with such programs and claim most parents are more committed to these programs since they are paid programs.

As a preschooler Luke attended the local children's rehabilitation centre. He did very well there but didn't want to be there for very long and Bob feels it's because Luke knew it was a 'special needs' school. Even though Bob says he has participated in integrated playgroups with his son Luke, he believes it would be valuable to have a playgroup/drop-in for developmentally challenged children and a support group for the parents: "…developmentally challenged kids have a tendency to play better together…as they grow up…[It's] just my perception.".

Bob and his wife have been offered Respite Services but have never utilized it since Bob is hesitant to leave his children with unfamiliar people. He prefers people whom he knows and anyway, he would rather be spending his time with his wife and children. Bob's outlook on life has been impacted by his own struggles with both alcoholism and over-eating. He is a recovering alcoholic and drug addict, and is a member of Alcoholic Anonymous and Over-Eaters Anonymous. Bob and his wife both attend the meetings, which he declares are technically "meetings" but also very social. They feel very comfortable and supported: "I can have an argument like most married people with my wife and go to a meeting and I share in a step and I listen to other people's recovery and how they're doing steps and by the time I leave my blood pressure is down...I like to say it's incredibly cheap therapy." And recently Bob has become a sponsor in Alcoholic Anonymous which is a great accomplishment.

Bob remembers growing up in a family where his parents were "really, really, really, really pushing him ...to be better then they were ...you know.... To have more than they did..." When it comes to his children and his expectations for them, he believes in encouraging them, not pushing them into doing anything they don't want to do simply because you expect them to. Bob feels that there are many damaged people who

were pushed to be the best they could be when they didn't feel capable, or have the tools and resources needed: "So that's my attitude with my kids...if they want to do something and we're financially capable of doing it...then they do it and if he does it three times and wants to stop...that's fine...I don't consider it failure... I consider that common sense. There are so many people out there today [who] do jobs they have to because they are told, 'You can't quit'... you know... 'You got to be productive'...but are you happy?" He doesn't perceive Luke ever holding a serious job and only wants him happy, to have fun, play, and enjoy life. He acknowledges, however, that his wife has a different outlook. She is more goal-oriented and pushes Luke to be the best that he can be.

Bob's expectations of his boys' school are that they teach his sons to read and learn good social skills. Because of Luke's 'special needs', he sees benefits and limitations to inclusive education for Luke. Bob would like him to participate with peers to develop his social skills to lead as "normal" a life as he can for as long as possible before his disease takes hold and becomes a determining factor in his life. He also prefers one consistent Educational Assistant for children with special needs rather than replacing the E.A. every year. His concern is that the children build trust and bond with the E.A and then the following year must learn to trust and connect with a new person. This makes it difficult for the child. He believes their job as parents is to teach their sons to respect other people and their property and he's hoping that the school will teach them how to act in a public environment. Bob explains,

"That kind of conditioning …he's going to need. If Luke is cognizant of his surroundings to the extent that he is only mildly…mildly mentally disabled….then yeah…I'm glad they're showing him the social skills he's going to need for being in public… If my son's mental age will never get over seven… I'm not going to expect much because chances are Luke will spend most of his time with special-needs children…"

On the other hand he is concerned that as Luke gets older other children will begin to ostracize him. He states,

"[This] is what hurts a parent's heart because you know he's yours, which is why we had the discussion of possibly, at some stage, to take him out of regular school and put him in a special-needs school because Luke had

the greatest time that we saw when he was in the rehabilitation centre."

Bob believes the school's expectations of them as parents in regards to their children are 'universal'.

"Whether he's disabled as Luke is or he's able as Mark is…I think a school's expectation should be that I get …my child there on time, that they're appropriately dressed and supplied,….that we're attentive to their school homework and that we ask them about their day …that we participate in school activities…"

Bob describes himself and Mary like "ying and yang." Mary will go on the field trips, give the boys medication and take them to appointments and birthday parties, which he refers to as the "official" participation, whereas he is the "physically active" one, loves to play outdoors, play soccer, watch TV, play video games, and just spend time together with the boys. Between the two of them they feel they have it covered. They are very interactive and involved with the school, communicating with the teachers, and talking with the boys when they come home.

In order for professionals to better service and meet the needs of his family, Bob emphasized the importance of being honest, understanding, attentive, and attempting to do the best that is within their job description both legally and emotionally. He believes most parents of children with special needs do not partake in enough courses and groups where they learn to deal with their anger. Therefore, conflict resolution or anger management classes would be valuable. Parents of children with special needs, he says, go through a lot of trauma and denial and he believes they would benefit from such programs.

Bob believes that doctors are reluctant to prescribe experimental drugs even if parents want to give it a try. He would like to see limited liability for the pharmaceutical companies. "At this point there are a lot of the drugs that the pharmaceutical companies ,,,are hesitant to try because of the side effects and [possibilities of parents] suing..." Also on his wish list, which he foresees as never happening, is for the federal government to prohibit the pharmaceutical companies from completely controlling the market. He stresses that for "pharmaceutical companies, a cure is useless.... A cure is a one time deal; it's more profitable to maintain a disease.... You know ....I remember I think it was ten percent of muscular dystrophies... there was only a ten percent success rate which of course is unacceptable for a pharmaceutical company. But I thought, you know, for the ten kids out of a hundred that it cures, that's a hell of a gift." He says his family could benefit from the "government cutting the red tape", for more openness from the government and pharmaceutical industries, as well as better education. "...because when you first find out, you want everybody to help you ...and you don't realize that the day you find out is the most horrible day and that's the most horrible year. Then you're just a person in line [and]....you know there are other families with Muscular Dystrophy..."

As a parent Bob finds his proudest moments with his children are quiet moments like putting his sons down for a nap, looking over and seeing them asleep. Watching them sleep for ten minutes and thinking, "That is the most perfect person I've seen in my life," or when they are sitting down next to him and look up and say, "I love you daddy." Those he considers the proudest moments because they are 'freely given'. All other things, like finally learning to put on their pants or go to the washroom, are progress in their life which they just learn. "The proudest moment is when your child gives you love unconditionally; you know it's worth it." The

Miller family has overcome adversity because they no longer think of it as adversity. It's just part of their life now. Luke has Duchene Muscular Dystrophy and "they do okay", they cope by taking one day at a time: "You can do anything for one day...it's only when we think about tomorrow and how long forever will be that we can become overwhelmed...so we're a typical family...we argue ...we laugh...we fight and we cry."

Discussion Questions:

> What impacts have Bob and Mary's backgrounds and experiences had on their beliefs and attitudes about their son Luke, who has special needs?
> How can parent-professional partnerships be encouraged between the Miller family and the health care services they access?
> How can teachers and schools respond to Bob and Mary's differing views of inclusive education for Luke?

The Sanford Family

A family with children with disabilities

The Sanford family lives in a small coastal Nova Scotian community. Ryan and Samantha ("Sam") have peacefully cohabitated in the town of Pembrook for the past twelve years, during nine of which they cared for four respectful children. Ryan identified himself as a stay-at-home dad responsible for raising and nurturing the couple's children: Harold, aged nine, Marie, aged seven, Douglas, aged six, and Louise, aged five. Ryan receives a disability pension which is their primary source of income. Sam is employed as a shocker at a local clam factory, earning minimal income, as she has done for the past seven years. Life has never been easy for the couple described as "retarded" and "slow" by staff of the Department of Community Services (DCS) the very agency they fear and try in every way to appease.

Sam is the eldest of five children born to Acadian and First Nations parents and self identifies as an Off Reserve Aboriginal woman. Ryan is the eldest of fourteen children and prides himself with helping his mom (often a single parent) care for his younger siblings to give her a break. Both Sam and Ryan have a daughter from previous relationships. Harold, the eldest of the four children whom the couple raises together is not Sam's biological son. The couple met when Harold was two years old. "Harold doesn't know [he and] the other children have ...different mom[s]; he thinks Sam is his mother."

Both Ryan and Sam are high school dropouts and were place in adjusted or modified (non-academic) programs during their junior high education. Their ability to advocate for themselves and their children is limited but they have received support and assistance from the Pembrook Family Resource Centre and the Tacoma Workshop (a facility/work program for physically and mentally challenged adults) over the years.

The DCS and the Family and Children's Services have been in the couple's lives for over a decade. Ryan reports the Agency first became involved with him when Harold was born in New Brunswick, at which time a file was opened with Family and Children's Services. When Ryan moved to Pembrook, Nova Scotia, with his son the file was transferred from the New Brunswick Agency to the Pembrook Agency. When Sam and Ryan began their family the couple had several visits from case workers with concerns that the children were not being looked after properly. The DCS identified the children as low functioning and having special needs as a result of being developmentally delayed. The parents disagreed with the Agencies assessment and felt the children were developing fine and are intelligent individuals.

Sam was approached by her social worker from DCS and asked to have her tubes tied to prevent her from having more children. The worker made the appointment in Halifax for the surgery and transported Sam for the scheduled procedure. Once Sam arrived at the hospital in Halifax, she decided to take the advice of her mother and not have the surgery.

A short time later Ryan was asked to have a vasectomy and as a reward the Agency would buy him a new bicycle. He was harassed repeatedly for a one-month period. Ryan agreed after getting a verbal promise from his case worker from DCS that his children would not be apprehended and placed in foster care. The appointment was made by a social worker at DCS and Ryan was transported to the Pembrook Outpatient Department and the vasectomy was performed. After the procedure he was returned home with a bag of frozen peas doubling as a cold compact to reduce the swelling from the surgery. As promised, the bike was purchased later that week and given to Ryan for his cooperation. "The Agency took my manhood away, nothing I could do about it; they did it and got away with it."

Approximately one month after Ryan's vasectomy the agency filed court proceeding to apprehend the four children and place them in foster care. The couple felt betrayed and they were extremely angry. Prior to filing court proceedings, the DCS suggested that four children were too many for the parents to manage and that Sam and Ryan should select two of their children to raise, and have a family member raise the other two. "We couldn't choose; they were not animals."

Sam and Ryan had taken several parenting programs at the Pembrook Family Resource Centre, and a Parent Skills Worker from the Tacoma Workshop provided individual counseling and hands-on skills training in the couple's home daily. Staff members were in the residence from early morning until 11:00 pm to teach the couple the art of parenting. The couple complied with every request and directive from the DCS.

After a lengthy court hearing, the judge awarded custody of the four children to Sam and Ryan and ordered that the supports and service remain in place until deemed unnecessary by DCS. Unhappy with the decision, the DCS appealed the judge's decision to the Supreme Court of Canada and won. "They classified us as unfit parents, half retarded; they said we weren't all there." All four children were apprehended and placed in a foster home in Pembrook. Two years later the foster family had Harold and Douglas removed from their care; they now reside together in a neighboring community.

Today Ryan and Sam are denied access and visitation with their four children by the DCS, yet they continue to love them. "We don't love one more than the other." That was obvious when they could not choose which ones to keep. It is the parents' hope and expectation that one day all their children will be successful professionals who will respect others, independent of their varying levels of ability and education.

Discussion Questions:

> Describe the values, attitudes, and assumptions about individuals with disabilities, which are the basis for the decisions made for this family? Do you agree/disagree?

> What are the family's strengths? How can service providers support the family's strengths and collaboratively problem-solve and make decisions for the family?

> Review legislation and human rights mandates in your jurisdiction which have an impact on the delivery of services to children with disabilities and their families. What ethical issues are raised in this narrative?

The Smith Family

A family with a child with disabilities

Noah is the second child of Jill and Brent, a young married couple who live in a small rural Ontario town. They have four children, Keith (8) from a previous relationship, Katie (4), Noah (3) and a new born, Kira. They live in the town core in a rental home, with family members, Jill's brother, his wife, and a family friend. At times the housing situation is over crowded. The adult family members work shift work, allowing the family to work out a schedule at home.

Jill has just given birth to her youngest daughter, Kira. Jill is planning to return to school in the next couple of months and has Kira on the child care waiting list. Jill's goal is to complete her grade 12, then enter the Personal Support Worker course at the local college. Brent is the night manager of a local fast food restaurant and works varied shifts to support his family. In the future Brent and Jill would like to have their own space and a place of their own.

Noah was born full term; after his birth the doctors informed Jill that Noah had one smaller and shorter leg than the other. Noah was diagnosed with Proximal Femoral Focus Deficiency (PFFD) which means he does not have a thigh bone in one of his legs. Noah is a very determined little boy who is able to get around quickly by crawling. He was fitted with a prosthetic leg about a year and a half ago which he uses regularly. He soon will need to be fitted for a longer one as he continues to grow and develop normally. Some parents may save their child's first tooth or lock of hair, but Jill plans on saving Noah's first prosthetic leg. "Who knows he may want to make a lamp out of it someday."

Noah prefers to participate in activities at home like watching television and playing computer games. He prefers to not wear his leg at home, as the family home is two levels, and it is difficult for him to maneuver the stairs with the leg. Noah has been involved with the child care center for more than three years. When Noah started at the local child care center, he was 8 weeks old. He wears his leg at the child care center and is able to participate in most activities to his fullest. Jill is encouraged that when Noah is eight or older, the doctors will perform surgery to give Noah a knee to allow for him to bend his leg.

Recently, Jill and Noah had a chance to attend a War Amps Conference in an urban city, an hour away. Noah originally was to attend the conference with Brent to have some "Daddy Time" but Brent was unable to attend, due to his work schedule. Jill wanted Noah to see other children with prosthetic limbs. She also wanted more information about a leg with a knee joint. One of Jill's dreams for her son is for him to ride a bicycle like his siblings do. He finds it is difficult to ride a bike, as his current leg does not bend, and he is unable to pedal. Jill is very knowledgeable about her community resources which help to meet her family's needs. The family does not own a car and is able to get around by walking with a stroller or wagon or by taking taxis or bikes. When Jill needs to go out of town for an appointment with Noah, she makes arrangements with War Amps and they provide taxi rides. Out of town appointments are in the local urban center which is a one hour drive away. Transportation is one of the major barriers for the family. "Because we live in such a rural area, it is so hard, there are no trains, there are no buses but one, that comes on Fridays. If you leave, you basically can't get back until next Friday."

The family uses formal services such as Ontario Works for child care subsidies, child care center, resource consultant program, occupational therapy and physical therapy, Board of Health, Assistance for Children with Severe Disabilities (ACSD: specialized funding to help meet any additional needs Noah may have), assorted doctors, and the local food bank. The family has received support from other community services, such as a Christmas Hamper program. They have accessed funding from a local church, for funding for glasses for Keith and Katie.

Jill is a very proud woman who will do what she has to do to meet her family's needs. She has a strong belief about how she would like to be respected by those providing support services. She believes service providers think they know what she needs. She would like service providers to ask her first before thinking they know what is best, and assuming because they are a family with a limited income, that they need handouts. An example she gave was one of the child care staff gave her a bag of clothes for Katie. The gesture was given in kindness but other parents could see the clothes with the note attached in Katie's child care cubbie. If the staff had asked Jill first, they would have known that she did not require any additional clothes for her daughter. When asked what she would like the staff to have done differently, she said, "Ask me what I need rather than assume you know what I need."

Jill is a very resourceful and resilient young woman. The family recently experienced the death of their young daughter Kira. In discussions with Jill, prior to this loss, we talked about what they would do if the family experienced a family emergency. Jill indicated she would call a family friend, seek help, and do what needed to be done. This was proven when the family experienced the loss of Kira. Jill used her network of informal supports to help the family through this difficult time. She has developed a close friendship with another parent with a special need's child at the child care

center. Jill used the informal support of her friend during the family crisis.

Noah will attend school next year, and Jill is starting to look at what needs to be done to make Noah's transition successful. When Jill first moved back to town, Keith started public school. The family has since had all the children baptized in order to attend the Catholic separate school. The reason she looked at the Catholic separate school system was because transportation is available to the school and the children are bused from her area. Jill foresees Noah having difficulties with getting on and off the bus and has considered contacting the bus company to see if arrangements can be made to get a bus with a lower access for Noah on the bus route.

When asked what she wants for Noah, she shared that she wants him to have a good life and have the same opportunities as other children. "I dream of - in real life, he would never be made fun of and he would be able to play with the other kids but, kids can be cruel and we live in that society." Having dreams and ambitions for our children is part of our role as parents. Jill has dreams for her four children, which reflect a strong sense of self worth and self respect.

Discussion Questions:

> What values and beliefs are priorities for this family?
> How would you as a professional approach and collaborate with this mother to reframe your services to meet her expectations?
> How can this narrative be used by the mother to reduce her vulnerability when approaching new services?

The Sorin Family

A family with a child with disabilities

Sitting quietly in the lounge of the child care centre attended by their three-year-old son Alexandre (Sasha), Anna, a thirty-five-year-old mother, and her husband Ilyia, fifty-two, told their family's story. They had decided to start Sasha in child care seven months earlier when his pediatrician suggested that this experience could benefit his development. Anna has been his primary caregiver, but she sadly describes the challenges they face as a family as it becomes increasingly clearer that Sasha is developmentally delayed.

Anna came to Canada seven years ago after she married Ilyia in Russia. Ilyia had immigrated to Canada many years prior to his marriage. Most of Ilyia's family and their family home had been destroyed in the first waves of the Chechnyan uprising. In Canada he holds a steady job in which he works long hours on varying shifts day and night. Before marrying Ilyia and immigrating to Canada, Anna worked and supported herself as a teaching assistant and enjoyed many hobbies in the arts. However, both she and her husband believed that they could offer their children a better life in Canada than in Russia, so they came to Canada to start their family.

They were devastated when, a year after arriving in Canada, their first son died fifteen hours after he was born because of what Anna describes as "poison in his blood". Their second son Sasha was eight pounds, six ounces, at birth after a healthy pregnancy and delivery by caesarian section. But at six months of age Anna became concerned that Sasha's legs were weak and his head was large. Assessments at the Hospital for Sick Children did not reveal any major abnormality. However, Sasha did not crawl until fourteen months and did not walk until eighteen months of age. Now at three years of age, he is described by his mother as walking only on tip toes, speaking only one- or two-word utterances in English and Russian, their home language, and demonstrating behavioural challenges particularly in changing environments. Extensive assessments by pediatricians and neurologists do not reveal any specific cause for his global delays; further genetic counseling and testing are being administered. Sasha's development is currently being supported by his mother, child care teachers, an early childhood resource consultant for children with special needs, and a speech and language pathologist. He is waiting to receive occupational therapy.

Although her husband and doctors keep reassuring Anna that Sasha will progress, Anna is very concerned that he is "slow" and will have to go to a special school, as this is looked down on in her country. She compares Sasha's development to the typical development of her friend's son. When she visited family in Russia last year her sister expressed concern about Sasha's development, but Anna is trying to hide her problems from other members of her family, as they are ill and so far away. She says that her friend in Canada and her sister in Russia are the only people that she can turn to for support. Her husband

works shifts at his job and often comes home too tired to play or interact with Sasha, although she is encouraging him to give the boy more play time. The family is currently receiving child care subsidies to assist them in providing Sasha with his early learning opportunities. Anna would like to work to assist the family with their finances but she is too exhausted providing for Sasha's daily needs and too afraid that she will not find a job that she can perform successfully in Canada. Anna feels alone with her problems and anxious about the outcome. This has contributed to her depression and inability to sleep.

When Sasha was a baby Anna attended a family drop-in with her friend who is also from Russia. She tries hard to promote his development at home by reading to him Russian books and playing with him. The family is Russian Orthodox, but as concerns about Sasha's development increase, Sasha's unusual behaviour makes it stressful for her to go to church with him. She tries to practice her religion at home although her husband is less observant. Anna has trusted Sasha's pediatrician to guide her to services within the medical system. In addition, the pediatrician referred Sasha to speech and language therapy and occupational therapy. The pediatrician recommended the family resource program which sent a special needs resource consultant to assess Sasha in their family home and who continues to support his progress in the child care setting. When Sasha first entered the child care program he had great difficulty with separations and would cry for hours when his mother left. Now he enjoys being at child care and the child care teachers have suggested ways in which Anna can encourage his independent feeding and dressing.

Anna describes herself as once having many friends but since Sasha was born her social and religious circles are limited. She relies on doctors for referrals, because, as she said,

> "...I didn't know anything about the KIDS community or service centre - even speech and language therapy; all [came] from Sasha's doctor. I didn't know anything. Sometimes I think I am very stupid. I was very useful in my own country, I knew everything about everywhere. But here I don't know

anything because first I am scared because my language is not very good, and I don't know if the information is helpful for me or very wrong. I am doing the best I can do. That's all."

Anna still hopes for a brighter future for Sasha. She believes that more individual attention is needed both in the child care and at home to support his development. She notes that while the teachers are excellent and he has progressed at their centre, they must divide their time among many children and Sasha needs more assistance if he is to be ready to participate and learn when he attends elementary school. Her hopes for Sasha are that he will become the same as other children, graduate from university, and have a good job which he enjoys. She hopes that the music he loves now will become a career path for him and that he will have the "better life" that she and her husband wanted for their family when they came to Canada.

Discussion Questions:

> What socio-cultural factors impact on the provision of services for children with special needs and their families?
> What expectations does Anna have for her child that effects service provision?
> What discrepancies may exist between a professional's view of success for Sasha and his mother's expectations for success?
> How can the professional's interactions with Anna and Ilyia be adjusted to accommodate their individual views?

The Spears Family

A family with a child with disabilities

Janet Spears is a thirty-four-year-old white Canadian female, born in a small Ontario town. She is married to Dave; they have a three-year-old daughter, Amanda. Janet was raised by her mother and step-father with four sisters and a brother. Janet lost contact with her biological father after her parents divorced when she was four, although she has resumed some contact in recent years. She considers her step-father her 'Dad' and his children from a previous marriage her siblings.

As a child Janet describes herself as being anxious when away from her parents and having a phobia about death. This began from the age of about five or six; Janet says she did not tell anyone about these experiences, although she continues to experience anxiety in her adult life. At thirty-eight, Janet's mother suffered a brain aneurysm and a short time later had a stroke during a surgical procedure to remove a second aneurysm. She is now confined to a wheelchair and cared for at home by her husband. At twenty-five Janet was diagnosed with fibromyalgia, resulting in limited physical energy, and at times "foggy" thinking and low concentration.

Janet met Dave in her hometown and married when she was twenty-one. At age thirty Janet had almost given up hope of becoming pregnant. She decided to accept a new job and had begun to discuss the possibility of adoption with Dave. Two weeks after starting her job, she found out she was pregnant. Janet, Dave, their friends and family were thrilled. This was a dream come true.

Janet describes her pregnancy as very positive up until the point of delivery. She had been ordered to quit her job and take it easy by the fourth month of her pregnancy because of high blood pressure, but this did not seem negative as she was so elated to be pregnant and looking forward to the birth of her daughter that anything she needed to do to care for herself and her baby seemed absolutely worth it.

After the cesarean birth of Amanda, Janet developed an infection in her abdomen that required several hospitalizations and medical treatments that were painful and restricted her movement. During the first few months after Amanda's birth it was difficult for Janet to provide physical care for Amanda without experiencing discomfort. Dave worked long hours to support the family but was able to support Janet during the evening and weekend hours. Janet describes Dave as a "huge support" and willing to contribute.

Amanda was diagnosed with torticolis when she was five months old. She therefore has unspecified muscle weakness, abnormal skull bone development, anaphylactic allergies to nuts, legumes, sesame seeds, and eggs, and an intolerance of milk and milk products. Amanda has a physical developmental delay of approximately one year. Emotionally she struggles with anxiety and has great difficulty separating from Janet.

The birth of Amanda was a time of celebration and joy for Janet and Dave. They were so thrilled with their new little "angel" and felt very blessed. Janet views her daughter's special needs as simply a part of who she is and not something to be disappointed about. Amanda is part of God's plan and Janet knows she can manage because God wouldn't give her more than she could handle.

Janet has a well developed professional support network to meet Amanda's developmental and medical needs. She spent a lot of time being visited by and visiting physiotherapists, child development workers, anxiety counselors and doctors. In general she has found these services to be supportive and respectful of the family's needs. She does experience some frustration with the lack of communication between professionals and a lack of information about how to navigate the variety of services. She says her biggest frustrations and challenges are those associated with Amanda's allergies. She feels that in general people do not take these issues seriously enough and that the allergies are the most "disabling" circumstance in Amanda's life. This is an issue she has across the board with professionals, friends, and family and even in the marriage relationship. Janet believes that others would like her to "be less protective" of Amanda but she sees herself as Amanda's advocate and identifies her role as a "preventer of problems" related to potential allergic reactions.

Janet's personal support network is less well developed and responsive to her social needs. Janet's needs for independent activities and adult relationships that are separate from the care of her daughter are only beginning to emerge. Up until now her husband has been the primary support available to Janet. This can be difficult as he often works long hours at a physically demanding job. In addition this impacts Janet and Dave's ability to find 'couple' time in their busy schedule.

The need for personal support is becoming increasingly important as Janet is planning to home-school because of her ongoing concern about Amanda's risks arising from her allergies. As a result the start of kindergarten will not be an opportunity to pursue some of her adult needs and in fact will add to her role as 'teacher' once Amanda turns five.

Amanda is a petit, curly-haired girl with dark, captivating eyes. She is quick to laugh and loves to share stories and her knowledge and to ask questions. Although withdrawn and quiet when she encounters new situations and meets new people, once she develops familiarity, she appears confident and is willing to participate in events and conversations with others. Amanda is very animated, playful and imaginative. She is an easily excited girl with a positive attitude toward life and many smiles to offer those she is comfortable with. Amanda is a 'watcher' of life and Janet noticed early on that she learns through observation before diving into something new.

Janet is so proud of Amanda for being so happy and having accomplished so much in her short life. Janet says that Amanda has already been through so much yet she is always happy. She sees Amanda as resilient and hopes that her enthusiasm for living continues forever. Janet wants Amanda to be "whatever she wants" and believes that Amanda's dreams "are Amanda's to have" and should not come from her. She will be there to enjoy and support her daughter in any way she can.

Discussion Questions:

1. In what ways can service providers and professionals demonstrate they are listening to this mother and understand her attitudes and views about Amanda's special needs?

2. How can the mother and father build on their strong relationship?

3. What value systems are demonstrated in this family's narrative? Is there synchrony between the family's values and beliefs and your own professional values?

The Whitehorse Family

A family with a child with disabilities

Sexual abuse and foster home care marked the teen years of Enid Whitehorse, a thirty-eight-year-old mother of five children. Enid lives in social housing in the downtown core of a large metropolitan city. Enid has two daughters, fifteen and thirteen years of age, and three sons, eleven years, four years, andseven7 months of age. Enid was born in Canada but at 3 months of age went to the Caribbean to live with her grandmother and later with her aunt and uncle. She recalls that when living with her aunt and uncle, her uncle was abusive towards her. When she was twelve years old, Enid arrived back in Canada where most of her immediate family already lived. She lived with her mother, father, and sister.

Enid was sexually abused by her father while her mother worked nights as a nurse. When she was sixteen years old, her father told her that he was going to impregnate her and she could be his second wife. Enid was terrified and confided this fact to a trusted high school teacher. The teacher took action immediately and that same day Enid was placed in an emergency shelter for young girls. Ironically, that same day her mother had her night shifts changed to day shifts at the hospital. But Enid did not return home, and until the age of eighteen, she moved from shelter to shelter. The first shelter asked her if she would like counseling and she said, "No".

At the age of twenty-one, Enid became pregnant and had a baby girl. But because of her past history she was considered high risk and the baby was removed from her care by the Children's Aid Society. Enid gave custody of her daughter to a relative. Two years later, Enid became pregnant with her second child and this child was also placed in protective care. Enid gave custody to the father's family to raise her second daughter. Without support or knowledge of her rights, Enid did not realize she had any alternative. Enid said,

> They figured that there's a cycle, that once you've been abused, you're gonna abuse your children. I didn't know any better – I could have gotten a lawyer involved, but I wasn't told nothing. I didn't know any better. So I just didn't want any problems...

Enid later had two sons with Carey who is of Native American Indian descent. This relationship lasted on and off for eight years. He was abusive throughout their relationship. When her second child by him, Sun, was four months old, she made Carey leave her home because of his threatening behaviour. Recently he was released from jail, but Enid has raised her boys on her own for many years and doesn't want him involved with them. The father of her infant son returned to Newfoundland and is not aware of his birth. She regrets that she did not raise her daughters as she has her sons and wishes she "knew what she knows now."

Two of Enid's children have special needs. Moon, eleven years old, and Sun, four years old, were diagnosed with speech and language delays. Moon was diagnosed at an early age since he was a late talker and when he did start to talk he had a stutter. Sun was diagnosed at age three. Enid describes Moon as very helpful and kind, but he doesn't like school. Sun, according to Enid, is shy, reserved, stubborn, and loves trains. Enid has been protector and advocate for her boys. When Moon was being bullied and mimicked for stuttering in one school, she tried to resolve the situation with the school. However, she did not feel she was getting assistance so she transferred him to another school where she believes the principal, teachers, and parents do communicate.

Moon received his speech and language services through the local hospital. Sun received services at a community family resource centre, and now at a school-based speech and language service. Enid found these services to be very helpful for both her and her sons. The therapists gave her suggestions and recommendations to assist her sons which helped their development. When Sun did not initially respond to the speech therapist, Enid allowed him to take a toy train to his therapy. One of her proudest moments was when Sun did speak to the therapist. Enid describes the moment, "...[The therapist] was all of a sudden...: Oh, you can talk! and

[Sun] kind of smiled; ...when he's interested in something his focus is on that one thing."

Enid has used food banks in the neighborhood, but was disappointed with them. The staff treated her unkindly and she has never gone back because they made her feel embarrassed. She found the food often has expired dates. One staff person told her that she should not have a phone and cable if she needs to use the food bank. Enid also attends a local drop-in centre and a local support group for single moms. She is very grateful to these staff for their helpful support.

Enid has health concerns. She was recently diagnosed with a disease called Devic's Syndrome, which usually attacks the limbs and eyes. The hospital and the doctors are not well informed about the disease. There has been little research on this disorder but her doctors tell her it is a "black" person's form of Multiple Sclerosis. Although she has lived in the same neighborhood for over twelve years and is happy living where she does because everything is conveniently located close by, she would like new accommodations. Her apartment is very small and only has two bedrooms. Enid has to sleep on the couch in the living room with the baby in a crib. As well, her building has no elevator and she lives on the second floor. With her disability it is often a painful experience carrying her young children, the stroller, and all their possessions up and down the stairs. She is additionally concerned about the amount of mould and holes in the wall while she waits a long time for repairs. Currently she is trying to get a larger apartment for her family in a neighborhood that will be safer from the drugs and crime in her present area.

Enid has completed her high school diploma and wishes to go back to school to study languages. She continues to be very proud of her children and their successes. She wants them to grow to be the best person they can be and to do whatever it is in life that they wish. This includes her daughters, one of whom has made the honour roll in school.

Discussion Questions:

> How have Enid's socio-cultural experiences had an impact on her beliefs, attitudes, and frustrations with educational, social, and health services?

> What are Enid's priorities for herself and her sons?

> Describe service delivery models that can support this family's healthy development.

> In what ways can services be reframed to reflect Enid's strengths?

The Ashol Family

A family new to Canada

Hannan Saleh, along with her four children and husband, left her home in Eminescun to try to find a better life for her family. As a refugee, she made the long journey with several other African families and separated from them in Toronto, with some of them traveling westward or staying in other parts of Ontario. Hannan and her family made the trip eastward and ended up settling into their new life in Newfoundland's capital city, St. John's.

Hannan and her family are adjusting to their new way of life but it has been very challenging to live in a place so dramatically different from where she came. The weather, housing, and traffic are some of the aspects of living here that at first were completely foreign to Hannan. However, her biggest and unexpected challenge after moving to Canada was facing life as a single parent. She and her husband had both enrolled in Memorial University but shortly after beginning her education, she was forced to quit due to an unexpected pregnancy. Her husband left her shortly after and got his own apartment while he continues to attend university. Hannan does not know what profession he is being trained for. While it is unclear as to how often he visits his children, when he does come, he is of great help to the children in assisting with their homework.

Hannan has taken some courses in English and is doing very well although there are times she finds the language barrier difficult, especially when dealing with professionals and service workers. Three of her children, aged eleven, nine, and five, attend school and are learning English through their classes. Her youngest is now sixteen months old and will learn the language through her family members until she too attends school.

St. John's is not generally considered a big city, but to Hannan, coming from a small village, living in a larger center restricts the freedoms she and her children had. She finds it very difficult to have to accompany the children everywhere they need to go, and in turn, feels very challenged in having to take four children with her when running errands. The fact that she does not have extended family members near is difficult for Hannan in several ways: not having any help with child care is hard, as is not having people around whom she loves and has close relationships with. Although she says she is happy to be living in Canada, she misses her family back in Africa a great deal. "I'm glad I'm here …but if we were here, all of them, than I would be glad a lot". Hannan manages to speak with her family members once or twice a month on the telephone. She feels very isolated and worries about her family's situation back in the Eminescun, where there is considerable civil turmoil. Her hope is one day to be able to work and save enough money to bring some of her family members to Canada, but she realizes that will take a long time to accomplish.

Even though settling in Canada has produced hardships and major adjustments in the Ashol family's life, Hannan acknowledges the benefits of living in this country. Education is extremely important to Hannan as she believes it is the key to her children having success in their lives and she is thrilled that they are getting the opportunity to attend school and study here. Living near adequate hospitals and having access to doctors is also a major benefit for Hannan and her children and she is very grateful for Canadian medical institutions. Accessibility to medical services is something new for her because the area of the Eminescun she had lived in provided no medical help unless the family had enough money to pay for the services. Hannan's family could rarely afford to get medicine or other assistance for their health. Their strong faith was all they had to rely on: "You just live and pray for God to bring health in your house." Monthly rental fees are paid for and after all her expenses are taken care of, there is not enough money for anything extra. She is very grateful for all the financial assistance she is receiving in our country, but feels that more understanding of families who have several children would result in more consideration being shown them.

Hannan and her younger children attend programs at a Family Resource Center and have met other families from Africa there as well. The FRC helps to combat her sense of isolation as well as assist with learning English. Her children enjoy attending school and receive extra help through a tutoring program. Homework can pose a problem because of the language barrier. Her sons are interested in playing sports and Hannan hopes to enrol them in some recreational programs this year.

Hannan is a very strong woman who is determined to make a better life for her children. Although she was born in Eminescun, she grew up in impoverished areas of Ethopia, mostly within refugee camps. Fleeing from rebels and violence was commonplace for Hannan and her family and she is proud that here in Canada, her children are safe and she doesn't have to worry about wars and overcoming obstacles to safety and survival. Her idea of success is for her children to learn and receive a good education, as well as to grow into caring and considerate citizens. Hannan believes that by living here in Canada, her children will have a better chance at living a good life.

Once her children are older, Hannan hopes to go back to university in St. John's where she plans to take education courses and become a teacher. Her dream is to return eventually to her home in Africa and share her knowledge by teaching poor children to speak English.

Discussion Questions:

> This family has lived in refugee camps for years. What do you see as the special needs of such families, and how can service providers distinguish between the needs of those who arrive as immigrants and those who arrive as refugees, the better to serve both groups?

> Education is of very high value to this family. Do you think there may be any connection between this and Hannan's husband's flight from his family to another apartment? Should this be investigated? If there is such a connection, for instance, if her husband sees a quiet room apart as the only way he can get the degree he needs to build a new life, is there a way this family could be supported in their educational aspirations short of such a separation? Should he have to make such a choice, if this is what it is?

> Hannan states that there is a need for more understanding of larger families, so that the services provided them (housing, etc.) are more

appropriate. Where would you as a service provider go to attempt to advocate on behalf of larger families, and how would you do so?

> Hannan is described as a strong woman. Whether she and her husband are every reunited, what do you see as most helpful in assisting this woman to build on her strengths and achieve her goals?

The Feliz Family

A family new to Canada

Abdi Feliz has two sons and wanted them to learn to "Respect people...respect other people's religion...be friends with your enemies. Afterwards, another time, [the enemy] would think, why would I hate this guy? –For nothing!" He wants his boys to learn about other cultures, and to make good use of opportunities offered by people from other cultures. For example, if someone from a different culture offers them a job, they should take it, and show them how good they are. Abdi says he would have no problem even if his sons wanted to marry someone from a different religion or culture. However, his wife adds she would prefer the same religion, not necessarily the same nationality. Abdi wants the boys always to listen to their parents and teachers, avoid getting a criminal record, and stay in school so

they can make something of themselves.

Trained as a laboratory technician, Abdi came to Canada seven years ago from Ghana, leaving behind a wife and a young son. A few years after his arrival he landed a job as a lab technician in a local hospital. Unfortunately, he was laid off when his hospital was shut down through government cut backs, and no similar jobs were available in other hospitals. Following a friend's lead, he eventually found a job in shipping and receiving at a department store, where he worked for three years. However, he lost his job again through company cut backs and now lives on social assistance.

Abdi lived frugally all these years, saving to sponsor his family. Nevertheless, it took five years for his wife and son to join him in Canada. Meanwhile, his wife Samia raised the boy by herself, with support from their extended family. Two years after her arrival another son was added to the family. For Abdi his proudest moment as a parent was "The day when we got …this young boy!"

Family and community are very important to Abdi. He says, "…my wife, my boys, all the time, if I go out, if I don't see them, I feel like I wanted to see them all the time." He thinks it is important for family members to listen to each other, to plan together (such as the family budget) and to acknowledge one's mistakes. He strongly believes "…you cannot do things by yourself" and that people achieve what they want only when they share their ideas and resources. Even to get a job in this country, he says, you need to have connections with people who have knowledge about job openings.

The family lives in a small bachelor apartment in a neighbourhood "infested with drug dealers and users, pimps and prostitutes." The parents worry when their older son is late coming back from school. The building in which they live is also badly in need of repairs but they cannot afford to move out. Their older son once got stuck in an elevator for two hours on his way back from school, which traumatized both the boy and his parents. Nevertheless, both parents claim to be happy and optimistic about the

future, especially for their children. Abdi believes, "When you are working, the money is not yours, it's for the kids. Back home, that's what we say, for the kids." This sentiment is based on parents being valued in the 'old country' for what they leave for their children, such as a farm, animals or houses. To fulfill this dream, Samia plans to take courses to eventually become a nurse. Abdi supports her ambition, claiming that when you have strong motivation to 'get ahead' you can do so. He is grateful to Canada for letting him live here, and Samia also thought that despite their current challenges, "…it will still be better here" than in Ghana, where she plans to go for a visit when she can, but not to live.

The family's primary challenges are financial. According to Abdi, "If you don't have money, there's nobody who can talk to you," and Samia adds, "If you have money then you're OK. If you don't have money then it's a problem."

The older son's education is another challenge for the family. When he first enrolled in a Canadian public school, he spent most of his time in the school playground rather than in class. Abdi found out that other children were also "just put in the playground, just play, and the teachers are just inside, they are just sitting. It is not the first time…" He found out that other parents had similar complaints about the school and eventually asked for his son to be transferred to a different school. Teachers in the new school answer all his questions and the boy makes good progress, especially in practical courses such as woodwork. Abdi initially tried to help his son with homework but found there were some things he himself did not know. The boy's teacher tried to help him in school but then the family found a tutoring program in the community, which the boy attends three times a week, with fare paid by the program, which is much appreciated.

For the younger son, the family has collected books and educational toys. He is taken regularly to a drop-in center, where "he sees all different people and things, like the computer. He just learns everything there, day by day."

Thinking about their long-term future, Abdi and Samia seem concerned about their isolation and abandonment by their children their old age, as the children integrate in Canadian society, get married, and move away. This was indicated by Abdi's detailed story about an old lady in this situation. He helped out by giving her some money, calling up her children, and eventually meeting two of them to convince them, "Back at home you have to respect your mother. You have to meet her even if she is unreasonable, to make sure she is OK." The old lady was eventually moved closer to where her children lived, and Abdi became friends with the entire family.

Discussion Questions:

> What are some of the key challenges for the Feliz family?
> What strategies might help the family address their challenges?
> What sort of a future do you think the Feliz children have, and why?
> Which policies and practices in Canadian institutions could help the Feliz family improve their chances of success?

The Gomez Family

A family new to Canada

Lena lives in a large rented farmhouse in rural Ontario. She has three children aged seven, five and three, and is shortly expecting twins. She and her husband Marco migrated to Canada from Mexico two years ago.

The family is deeply religious and traditional in their life style. They try to live a simple life, and avoid using technology, if they can. For example, they do not have a television at home because they think it would influence their children's ability to distinguish between what is real and what is not. They have a telephone and a van, but Marco's primary mode of transport is a bicycle.

The family speaks a language that does not have a written form. However, the family members have also learned Spanish and are now in the process of learning English.

Upon arriving in the area they first rented an apartment in town but soon found it to be too expensive, and not suitable for their family. They themselves felt "caged" and had to constantly tell their children to be quieter so they would not bother the neighbours. They thought their children were not listening very well and becoming somewhat "wild."

The family had to wait for a long time for Marco to get work, as he initially did not have landed immigrant status. Lena could not work because their culture did not permit women to be the primary wage earner. However, they received a great deal of support from the local community, but were uncomfortable recipients of what they perceived to be charity. Although they were not able to save money while they were still living in Mexico, they always had enough food and did not feel dependent on anyone.

When the opportunity to live and work at a farm became available, the family moved quickly. They rented the farmhouse for $250, paying part of the rent by working in the yard and feeding the horses. Their children now had more room to play and run around.

Lena and Marco initially enrolled their older son at the local public school but they did not approve the extensive use of computers and television in the school, which they believed over-stimulated their son; he started acting out at home and they attributed this to such stimulation. They subsequently moved him to a religion-based school, where values closer to their own were espoused and promoted. Their son was making good progress in the school and was at grade level in everything except reading. The family also began to attend a church that matched their belief system, specifically that of valuing one's children and making time for them. A neighbouring family provided some clothes for their son and had also offered support and friendship. However, Lena said that she, like many others in her community, continued to be fearful of the Children's Aid Society because she has heard of families' experiences of their intervention. She believed families needed to raise their children according to the teachings of the Bible and that child-rearing should not be a concern of the government.

Marco made buggies for a living. He started out by working in construction but found working outside in the winter quite dangerous. Furthermore, construction work did not give him sufficient time to attend to his family's needs.

Lena worked at home. She said she was trying very hard to be content with the work she did inside the house, but it was not something she naturally liked to do. She knew how important it was for a family to have a clean house, especially in the winter when they stayed indoors, and she was trying to teach her children to pick up after themselves. She came from a farming family and loved being outdoors. Her favourite activity was to pick vegetables while talking to other women as they worked. Her husband was not comfortable with formal education but she would like to pursue it and perhaps someday become a nurse, pharmacist or midwife. She had attended classes three days a week at the local community centre for learning to read and write English, health and nutrition, and parenting. She enjoyed the opportunity to interact with others and had reduced her visits to once a week only because of her advanced pregnancy.

Lena also wanted her children to

get a good education and choose whatever they want to become. She was proud of how quickly her children had learned English and how well they were able to do their school work.

The family had not decided whether to stay in Canada or go back to Mexico. They found the winters hard, and Marco's poor health did not help. However, they thought it was peaceful here; people were helpful and looked for the good in each other. In Mexico they were financially better off but people in general were not as supportive. Language was still a bit of a barrier in Canada. Lena thought her children may find it difficult to adjust to a Mexican school as they are not so well regulated, and she feared they may be bullied or ridiculed there. She said she would consider home schooling if they decided to return to Mexico. Both Lena and Marco came from large families and Lena often missed her extended family. One of her sisters had married one of Marco's brother in the same ceremony as their own marriage. The two couples were close and Lena still missed their company.

Discussion Questions:

> Do you think the Gomez Family should stay in Canada or go back to Mexico?

> What do you see in the family's future ten years hence, should they choose to stay in Canada?

> What supports, if any, should Canadian institutions offer to the Gomez family? How do you think they would respond to such offers?

The Kumar Family

A family new to Canada

Sita lives in a bachelor apartment in Toronto with her husband Manoj, five-year-old Ravi and two-year-old Sunil. Both Manoj and Sita have MBA degrees from a well-known university in India. They decided to immigrate to Canada so their children could benefit from good quality higher education. The immigration process took over four years, used up all of their savings, and led them to move in with Manoj's parents in Toronto. Currently, Manoj works the day shift at a nearby Wal-Mart, and Sita does the night shift from 10.00 p.m. to 7.00 a.m. She leaves for work after putting the children to bed and returns before they wake up.

Speaking of her children's future, Sita says that, like all parents, she wants the "the best" for her children. To her, this means "good health, education, [a] good position in society,

[and] much money." She says, "That's the main [reason] we came here...We work hard so we can get our children whatever they want, like new dresses or toys or whatever. When we were small children we didn't have so many expectations; ...we didn't want so many toys. But when you become a mother you think, whatever I didn't have, I want my children to have. Money is the basis for everything, isn't it?" She also emphasizes she wants her children to be have "a good character" which for her means, "He should be a family type of person. He should respect his parents. Most people in developed countries don't have that: [there is] no respect for relationships. I don't want my children to be so. I should always feel that they are my children. They should stay with me. I am a typical Indian (laughs)." She worries that the independence encour-

aged in Canadian society and all the different kinds of people and situations that her children would encounter, which she herself had not experienced and doesn't understand, could "lead them to the wrong road." She offers addiction to alcohol or drugs as examples of this.

Sita believes that parents, teachers, peers, the community, and the children themselves are responsible for building their moral character. She says, "I do believe in God and that spirit gives me and my husband strength to stay. I told you that we went through so many bad times, and I want my children to have that spiritual strength. They have to believe in God. ...I always teach [Ravi], we are a Christian family, so I tell him stories about Jesus Christ. I tell him there are angels to guard you when you fall down." Encouraged by acquaintances, she has enrolled Ravi in a Catholic school. She says, "I don't have a good communication with the church here so the school will teach him."

Speaking of herself, she says, "When I am in the apartment... I feel too bad, because I feel I am all alone." She misses her extended family's role in raising her children. She says, "Over there you have family, over here there are only two people. So it is difficult. So we have to play all the roles, mother, father, grandmother. Sometimes when [Ravi] wants to play

I have to do that too and [still] carry on the housework and working." Because of her sleep deprivation, she finds this particularly difficult. She says, "When I am in an angry mood, I don't want to go out and play with them, but I have to. It is very, very hard." She worries that she will not be able to teach her values to her children, and that she does not have extended family members or close friends to reinforce those values. She thinks this will be a greater challenge when the children reached their pre-teens and have greater independence.

Sita says her children enjoy Christmas in Canada because unlike in India "Here everyone celebrates Christmas." However, special occasions are difficult for her and her husband because they are away from family. Furthermore, social interactions with other adults are difficult because, "The problem is, morning he works and nights I work so we can't go anywhere. Even [yester]day, my husband was saying, if we go on working like this the children will not enjoy much. Even Saturdays, Sundays he has to work. Two or three friends called us to go to Niagara Falls but we couldn't go."

From her acquaintances, Sita is gradually learning what to buy and where. She said, "There is a family in the next tower and they told us how to meet the expenses.... We didn't know children had to drink homogenized [3.5 milk fat] milk and we bought 2% ...but then these people ...advised [us] to buy it, so we did; and for a 4 litre pack it is $4.99 here, but at Thorncliffe when we go it is only $3.79....We need more milk because of our younger [son]. Even if we spend subway money it [is] still worth it." When asked if she had tried food other than Indian food, she said, "No but I tried the fruits. I had never seen a pear before; we don't get it back home. ...Even cantaloupe I had at my friend's house and that was good." However, she could not afford some of the fruit her family used to have because, "I want some but when I see the price I say no."

Sita says her husband Manoj was initially conflicted about working at Wal-Mart and felt "very bad" because it was unskilled labour. However, the family needed the money and they were told, "'...getting a job in Wal-Mart is good and every job in Canada has equal value. Whoever works and earns money is respected in society.' So

they advised us like that. It's expensive, so only if you are working is [it] okay."

On a more positive note, Sita says that living in a diverse community was helping her children learn to be friendly. People greet them in the elevators and strangers are sometimes very helpful, such as the bus drivers who provided detailed directions for them when they first arrived. However, it was difficult to meet members of their own linguistic community because they didn't have a car until just two weeks ago, and finding time was always a challenge.

Sita hopes her children's school would provide them opportunities to participate in sports and art activities. Unlike in India, she believes her children have a wider choice of careers when they grow up, and opportunities to nurture their talents. She appreciates the interest teachers take in her children, and resources such as parks close to her building. However, for now she just wishes she had affordable child care available.

Discussion Questions:

> Are Sita's aspirations for her children realistic? Why or why not?

> What are Sita's resources and how can she use them to help her integrate in Canadian society?

> How can you as a professional collaborate with Sita to guide and support her with future decisions she must face for herself and her family?

The Saleh Family

A family new to Canada

Khamisa and Deng were married twenty-three years ago in Sudan. They moved first to Egypt for three years, and from there they moved to Canada in 2003. Alice described their decision to leave as based on the fighting in their country, the death of her parents, and the threats to their lives in Sudan. Her husband worked for the British Embassy at that time, and working for foreigners was causing others to threaten them. Their three sons immigrated with them; Zekara, who is now twenty, Hassan, now eighteen, and Mana, now eleven years old. They landed in Ontario and moved to Oshawa. Deng was able to find work in the automotive industry, and Zekara, her eldest son, was able to find work in the construction trades.

Deng and Khamisa were able to take some English as a Second Language (ESL) courses in Ontario, but the funding for these classes soon ran out. Thankfully, Deng already had some English skills, because of some time he had spent in Uganda. Deng trained as an accountant in Sudan, but needs a few courses before becoming accredited in Canada. He has been unable to take these courses because of the shift work job that he was able to find. Khamisa enjoys living in Canada, and is especially appreciative of the education and job opportunities here compared to Eminescun, especially for women. She explained, "In Canada… [there is] security…and [a] good life …because…you go to school…. In Sudan, you marry, no go to school."

In 2008, Khamisa and her two youngest sons moved to Alberta in search of a job for herself, and the chance for an economically better life for their family. Deng and Zekara hope to join the family in Alberta in the summer. Khamisa has found a job cleaning at night, and Hassan financially contributes to the family income with his after-school job. Because of the expense of housing in Edmonton, they live in the basement of their cousin's townhouse. They hope to be able to afford to rent an apartment one day.

The family continues to be close, despite the distance that separates them. They are all looking forward to the summer, when they can be together again. Khamisa is also looking forward to having her husband and oldest son join them, as Alberta Health Care will not insure the family until the family is living together as a unit. She cannot register her son for school in the fall until she has an Alberta Health Care number. This has been causing her much anxiety this spring. Despite the assistance of other Sudanese friends and community workers, she has not been able to change the minds of the Alberta Health Care staff or the school.

Khamisa and Deng's children have adjusted to Canada in different ways. Zekara, the oldest, has had the hardest adjustment to coming here. He did not speak a lot of English and still remembers life in Sudan. He likes to sing and play guitar, and hopes to create a CD of Sudanese and Arabic songs in English. He also plays soccer. He would like to go to university, but struggles because of his insufficient knowledge of English. He often speaks of returning to Sudan.

Hassan, the middle child, is quiet and introspective. He likes to play soccer as well, but would rather spend time at the church and reading. His English skills are fairly good, which allows him to have a part-time job to help his family. He has been able to catch up fairly well in school, and is now in high school. He has been able to develop many friends in Canada.

Mana, the youngest, started school in Canada, and has had little difficulty transitioning to Canadian life. He takes part in activities on Saturdays at the local Boys and Girls Club, including a homework club and recreation activities. Khamisa's cousin's sister-in-law drives the children to the Boys and Girls Club, and works for the local newcomer centre as a Sudanese community leader. Khamisa likes to walk her son to school when she can, but Mana does not always appreciate it. Mana does very well in school, and has received awards for his mathematics studies. This makes Khamisa very proud. Mana hopes to be a fire fighter or preacher when he gets older.

Recently, her youngest son had a problem at school, where he was kicked by another boy. Khamisa was able to talk to the teacher. They both agreed to have Mana's desk moved so that he was not close to the boy who wanted to fight, and they encouraged him to ignore the other boy; this ended the problem. Khamisa felt supported by the school, and has not had concerns with the education system here. Khamisa mentioned that the ban against spanking in Canada worries her as a parent. She is afraid that she will not be able to manage her children without spanking. She has not had too many problems with this, however, because of the ages of her children when they came to Canada.

Khamisa is not aware of many of the organizations that could help her family yet, as she has only been in Alberta for five months. However, they have strong family connections and a strong faith connection to their Christian church. She remarks on the importance of their faith, and that family togetherness times often include reading the bible together. Many of their social activities are weddings, funerals, and other activities through the church. She tries to help her children develop a strong faith as well, and would be happy if they could find wives who also believed in God. "So you want to teach them about God and....about being good people...."

Khamisa continues to keep their family's Sudanese culture alive by singing and reading newspapers and talking in their language to her children. She believes that when her children are grown, she may return to the Sudan, if there is some peace.

Discussion Questions:

> Thinking about three specific types of policies this family has encountered, how would you advocate for improvements in the areas of language training, health insurance, and professional upgrading? Why? How would this benefit both newcomers and Canada as a whole?

> What programs and organizations would be useful for this family to be connected with? What would be the best way to ensure such connections in the early stages of a family's life in Canada?

> This is a mature family with a lot of experience. How would you attempt to assist them to share the benefits of their experience with other Canadians, other than through employment?

The Momin Family

A family new to Canada

Friends and relatives envied Efem and her husband Yusuf, and called them 'a dream couple' while they were living in Nigeria. They were both highly educated: she had a master's degree in mathematics and he was trained as a chartered accountant. Both worked in banks, he as a top executive and she in a senior position in marketing. But things changed when their children began to arrive.

Adamo was eighteen months when he started going to a private nursery school. His doting parents and grandparents played with him, sang to him, and marvelled at each of his accomplishments. At the age of two-and-a-half, however, he began to lose his hearing as a result of a vaccination. His parents spent all their savings and then borrowed money for his treatment in the UK and Ireland, where they were told he was profoundly deaf in one ear and severely impaired in the other. They then applied to move to Canada, hoping his treatment and rehabilitation costs would not further drain the family's resources. Meanwhile, they had two more children, both girls, now three years and eighteen months old.

The family decided to live in a town where they knew another family from Nigeria. Efem did not think this was a good choice because the supports available for Adamo were limited in this town. They arrived in Canada in July but had to wait until September to enroll him in school. People at the school referred them to an agency where they were told about various options for his rehabilitation. It was recommended that Adamo be taught sign language, but the parents insisted that he should be taught oral language first, so he could communicate more easily. It was also recommended that he be moved to a special school for deaf and hearing impaired children, which was in another city. At first the parents resisted the idea of sending their boy to a residential facility, but they also found it difficult to cope with his behavioral problems and finally agreed to let him go. He now comes home only for weekends, and has to be picked up and dropped at a meeting point for the school bus.

Before they arrived in Canada, Efem and Yusuf thought it would not take them long to find appropriate jobs. However, they found that "You don't get much help beyond the forms you get upon arrival. You are lost. If you happen to arrive at the home of a person who is not well connected, he really cannot help you. If you stay with a cab driver, you end up being a cab driver. They say 'You want to make ends meet? You better get a cab and start driving.' And you may never learn that you can go back to school." She added "And the bills, they keep coming."

Renting a home was like 'money down the drain' for the family. However, when they wanted to purchase a home, they were asked to make a 50% down payment as they did not have a credit history in Canada. Getting a car was similarly expensive, but they could not do

without it, as the children had to be taken to school and child care.

Yusuf had now come to terms with the fact that it would take him three to four years to get retrained for the kind of job he wanted. Meanwhile, he had decided to sell insurance, working up to fourteen hours a day, traveling to different cities. Efem first stayed home with the children, but now that Adamo iss settled in his new school, and the girls are in day-care, she has enrolled in a technical college to qualify for teaching mathematics.

As a result, her routine has become quite hectic, especially as Yusuf is often away from home, traveling for work. She is up early to get the children off to child care, then do the housework and her school assignments, pick the girls up and drop them at a friend's place, and rush back to class which went on until 7.00 or 7.30 p.m. She is finding the school work challenging, but also interesting. She says, "Education is good here. We didn't learn about how to do presentations until we were in university. But we are doing it now." There are other things she is still discovering. For example, she finds the books very expensive, including one that was over three hundred dollars, but she recently learned that she could buy used books instead. "You have to get to hear it from people you know…because I didn't get to hear it before. I didn't even know you could apply for Ontario Student Assistance Program (OSAP)."

Efem has also found her children's education to be quite different. She said, "[My older daughter] is learning so many things in the day care, especially manners. At home [Nigeria] it is quite different. Playing? No. Teach them one, two, three (addition and subtraction)." She thinks her children have settled quite well in Canada already. "You can see their tradition has changed already, they are Canadians… they love it here." When asked if she and Yusuf have also settled down, she says, "NO! Not yet to settle, as in settle…and be as confident as we were in Nigeria. No, we have not yet settled."

Discussion Questions:

> Do you think the Momin's family decision to migrate to Canada was a wise one? Why or why not?
> What do you think about the decisions made by the Momin Family regarding their son's education?
> What can Canadian educational institutions do to support the Momin Family?
> What does it mean to really "settle"?

The Parkes Family

A family new to Canada

Valerie Parkes is a thirty-seven-year-old Caucasian woman born and raised in England prior to moving to Canada in April 2007. She is married to Kenneth, who was born and raised in Montreal and lived in England for ten years. With their two daughters aged eight and three and their son, aged eight months, Valerie and Ken arrived in Canada with all their belongings. Ken had obtained a job as a computer IT director and began work immediately while Valerie remained at home to provide the day-to-day care of the house and children.

Valerie started the ball rolling by suggesting the move to Canada. They thought Canada would offer a better work environment for Kenneth (regular hours and less traffic to commute in), more outdoor and sporting opportunities for the family, and a better education. They felt Canada offered a better way of life in terms of attitudes and opportunity. This was to be a time to focus on family and spend more time together.

Valerie felt sadness when reminiscing about their dreams and expectations of moving to Canada and how different it is from reality. " I think if we had done it how we were supposed to do it... but then things went against us like exchange rates and house prices... so it is not quite how it is supposed to be....I am almost in that same situation as I was in England but poor and with no friends...." Valerie has felt lonely in her new city and thought making friends would have been much easier than it has proven to be. She has had to learn about the school and health care systems on her own and still feels bewildered some of the time. For example, she was quite shocked to learn that within Canada, her daycare and child care needs were not paid for by the government. This system is very different from what she was used to in England.

Valerie found herself socially and emotionally isolated in Canada, as she misses her friends and family deeply. "...[It] is quite hard...it is tricky, really. So although I didn't have help as such in England, like some people around town, I had a bit of a support network so you could always ring somebody in the evening or get in the car and go and drive to somebody's house....You know, there's people I have known a few years [but] here if you've got worries or whatever, you can't just offload on somebody you don't know or you don't know well." Valerie finds herself with a social network made up of acquaintances and she does not feel as if she can unload her problems on them. She is hopeful that this will improve over time.

Valerie anticipated the children's school would lead to social connections for herself and her children. She imagined parents meeting at the school and making plans for coffee once the children began their day; she did not anticipate line-ups of cars and school buses with no opportunities to speak to other parents.

She values the importance of being a child and having an opportunity to play and explore. This is why she enjoyed the church play groups offered in many churches in England. These drop-in play groups are run by volunteer parents where tea and cookies are offered in a room full of toys with chairs for parents to visit with one another for a small fee. It is a time for parents to socialize and a chance for their children to get together. There seems to be no equivalent offering in her new community. The programs that are offered often cost money and seem expensive to Valerie. Further they seem to offer poor quality programming for the price they are charging.

Everything seems so different to her and she does not know what the standards are for education and health care. Valerie did not access services with the local immigrant society because she believed the focus was on immigrants who did not understand English and who needed a place to learn a new language. She wished there was some network to connect her with other new immigrants from England who might be experiencing some similar struggles and concerns as herself.

Valerie is very proud of her children for how well they have adjusted to their new life in Canada. Valerie is especially pleased with how her oldest daughter has adjusted and adapted to the school system and is making friends, while successfully completing her studies. Her oldest daughter is very helpful around the house and with her siblings, although Valerie is clear that she does not want her to assume too much caretaking responsibility. Her son is still very young and Valerie only expects him to be a child and to learn through play. Valerie believes her three year old the most challenging to parent with her strong ideas and persistent nature. However, Valerie values this strength of character and imagines how this will serve her daughter well in years to come.

She hopes that her children will enjoy their childhood and learn to follow the rules and expectation around them. She wishes that they could grow up without any serious problems and just be "normal" children; to be popular and to have a lot of friends. Valerie wants them to learn to work well with others, because this would be positive for them in life and she would feel some success as a parent if they accomplished this. She hopes they will work hard to have all they need, but balance their work and family needs, and perhaps contribute to their community (e.g., charity work). "I would like them to be caring and know right from wrong and do the right thing…just be a good friend to their friends and a good sibling and be a good person in the community and maybe do something, charity work…I think you have to strike the right balance really – like work to pay for the things you want but then again don't throw everything into work."

Discussion Questions:

> As Valerie's native language is English, she doesn't have some of the problems communicating that other immigrants may have, but she has the same problems that Canadians have who move for employment to a part of the country where they know no one. Is there some way that service providers can offer a means of integration into each community for newcomers through the schools their children attend? What would you recommend, and why?

> In previous eras, immigrants frequently found a place in their community through their local religious house. This is less common today, so for newcomers who do not have school-aged children, what would you recommend as a substitute base for connecting, other than the local school? And how could this be organized?

> At the moment, Valerie is a stay-at-home mother who feels that they are experiencing poverty. What would you advise Valerie to do to build upon her own strengths?

The Nadarajan Family

A family new to Canada

The Nadarajan family left their comfortable life in Sri Lanka to come to Canada to escape the political instability and high crime rate there. Indira Nadarajan and her husband Shyam Nadarajan, both well educated and professionals in their fields, have two young sons, Arun, five years old, and Wishal, three years old. They left Sri Lanka in 2005 when Wishal was only eight months old. They arrived in Canada with very little money and a list with of goals they hoped to achieve in their new home town.

A month after their arrival, Shyam found a good job in an established firm. They found a rental apartment close to work but Shyam was working long hours and studying to take his exams to get his CA; Indira was left to take care of the rest. "So I'm the one who has to look after everything, my two kids, and taking them to school... [and] we didn't have a second car... Suffering, suffering... in the winter, you know: going to another place to do shopping with two kids and the bus, going, coming, and carrying all those [things]. My small one was only eight months. But it's okay, our goal is to go much higher."

After two years Shyam received a substantial increase in his salary and the Nadarajan family decided to buy their own home: one of the goals set before their arrival to Canada.

Indira said they had not faced many challenges coming to Canada. "It's not difficult ... actually it's good, for in every way,... job wise, ...education wise, ... if we have some problem we can overcome it." Indira said that her son has been faced with a little racism but she felt that this is only a minor problem. The overall benefit for Indira was, "We are now in a better country in the world."

Shortly after the arrival of the Nadarajan family, Indira began attending playgroups where she met people and where she found out about other services. "I got lots of friends from there and talking to everybody you get more information from there." She said, "It's really worth those programs. I really appreciate it." It is from these services that Indira and her friends have now formed their own 'ladies night out.' "I got everything from these programs."

Wishal and Arun are both attending a public French Immersion school. When they are not in school, Indira is busy taking them to swimming class, parks, Aquarium, and other public children's sites. Indira spends her free time with her boys, studying and looking after her family. She does not have much time for herself. "I'd like to go for a walk but I don't have time. If I'm going, then I have to take my kids."

Indira attends more recreational activities but said that if the government-run agencies were to provide something, it should be free child care for those parents who are in school or continuing to study. And the care they provide should be more academic, alongside the play-based theory. She also stated that more information is needed regarding the types of government assistance and this information should be in the various child care settings: playgroups, Mother Goose, child cares, all the programs geared for young children. She also said that the facilitators of the various centers should focus also on trying to integrate newcomers to the center by trying to understand the needs of the participant rather than focusing only on the center itself.

Indira believes education is very important. Her expectations of her sons are to study hard. "I want them to study, study hard and be a good person." She also believes that the school her boys attend has high expectations of the children. "That is why I drive them every day [for a] half hour." To support her sons' learning and development, Indira takes time out from working and studying for her CGA exams to take a French class to assist her boys in their studies.

Indira feels communication with the school, playgroups and other public services is very important for the success of her children. In order to gain her trust, "they have to behave like a professional ...they have to be same like us." Success for Indira is shown when her sons have been able to grasp the values that she and Shyam have been trying to instil in them. "When they [sons] understand some points [values], we feel kind of happy;" and in school, it is when they have really understood the problem — as Indira says, "knowing the process rather than [just] the outcome."

Indira would like her sons to be good people, to be understanding and giving, within limits. She says "Whatever you get, be happy with that." She also feels that regardless of status or race, if you want to do something, you can. She truly believes that "if there is a will, there is a way."

The Nadarajan family is pleased to say that they have achieved all the goals they set on that piece of paper before arriving to Canada three years ago, and for Indira, her pride is her family. She is trying to keep her family happy. "I'm keeping everybody satisf[ied] … everyone's expectations … that's the …hardest thing, but we are doing it."

Discussion Questions:

> What, in your view, is Indira's contribution to Canadian society?
> What is Indira's role in supporting her family? What support does she herself need and how can this be provided?
> Is there a role public services could play in facilitating Indira's settlement in Canada? And if so, what would that look like?

The Dengu Family

A family new to Canada

Emil and Nadia both grew up in rural Romania, surrounded by extended family. As is often the case, both their parents worked, and Emil and Nadia were raised by their respective grandparents. They met at university and have been together for fifteen years. They have been married for four years and have a son, Mihai, who is twenty-two months old. Frustrated by limited job opportunities, Emil and Nadia applied to come to Canada to find work related to their fields of studies. Emil obtained his degree in aeronautical engineering and Nadia in sociology. After searching on the internet and making inquiries, they concluded Quebec might welcome them because they spoke French and had a good education. They studied together to learn about Canada, and made the three-hour drive to Bucharest to take the test and to be in-terviewed as prospective newcomers. With family help and their own personal savings, they were able to raise the required money to be accepted. A contact in Montreal found them an apartment, and they arrived with a sense of adventure and the hope of a promising future.

The challenges turned out to be far greater than they expected, and it is a testimony to their partnership that they can both say, "Now life is good." Their first apartment was depressing and unacceptable and they moved as soon as they could. Emil realized he needed to take any job that would make ends meet while he looked for a job as an engineer. He also realized he could improve his chances by having Canadian educational credentials. He found a certificate program related to his field at a French CEGEP, and was also resourceful in finding funding to subsidize the tuition. He gave up his job delivering pizza and took a different job that allowed him to be free during the day.

Every morning, Emil and Nadia were out of bed before dawn to deliver 600 morning newspapers before 6:30 a.m., at which time Emil headed off to school. It was difficult to study in French, but it helped him become more fluent in the language. Their first Christmas in Canada was lonely without the fanfare they had experienced at home, especially since Christmas was Nadia's birthday. With anticipation of better things to come, they managed to make the celebration special.

The second Christmas was even harder: things were moving slowly, their plans were not materializing, and they had not obtained jobs in their field. Emil and Nadia decided to move to Toronto to join his brother, who had come to Canada at the same time. Emil's brother was making good money as a truck driver and he convinced Emil to try it out. "Driving a truck was very hard. I was talking on the phone a lot because I missed my family. I was away for long periods and I missed my little boy." But "I drove all over the country. Now I feel more Canadian!"

In Ontario, however, the cost of living was higher than in Quebec, and since the aeronautical companies were centred in Montreal, they decided they were better off returning to Quebec. With persistence and luck, Emil was recently hired at Bombardier. Although he is working at a job below his level of training, he appreciates the opportunity to work in his field, and hopes in time to be able to move up. Nadia has also found a job with a very good boss, and although she would like to do better for herself, she is satisfied for the moment.

Emil and Nadia are creating an environment for their son Mihai that reflects their own Romanian culture and incorporates their new Canadian way of life. They speak to him in Romanian and want him to learn English as well as the French he will acquire at school. He will be going to a bilingual child care centre (English and French), and both parents wonder how best to encourage language development. Should they speak to him in English or continue to speak to him in Romanian and hope he learns English in child care? Although Mihai is very young, they share memories of their childhood with him through stories, songs, food, and celebrations. Emil and Nadia were raised in families that had been members of the traditional Orthodox church, but once the Communists had taken over (in 1945), religious practice had been discouraged. They have not joined any church here in Canada and feel confident about imparting their own moral values to their son as he is growing up.

Education is valued in Romania. University is free but students must work hard to earn the privilege of good schooling. It is important that their son Mihai be successful in school, but the most important thing is that he be happy. Right now they worry about him because he is 22 months old and has only a vocabulary of about six words in Romanian. They were extremely concerned he might have autism. Since obtaining some help from a speech pathologist a month ago, however, they have seen encouraging changes. They have focused their attention on Mihai,

playing with him and stimulating him, and the results show evidence of a smart little boy who is playful, responsive, curious, and affectionate, and most likely not on an autism spectrum. They have used the internet to find resources, and are looking into different possibilities for helping their son with his development.

Since making the decision to leave Romania, Emil and Nadia have supported each other through the challenges of starting a new life in a foreign country, having a baby, and worrying about that baby's health. Finally, after three years in Canada, they are satisfied with their successes, and are optimistic about their future here.

Discussion Questions:

> Why do you think it was so difficult for Emil to find a job at an appropriate level in the aeronautical industry?

> Do you think Emil made the right decision in taking a pre-university level course in aeronautics?

> What do you think about the parents' decision to expose their child to multiple languages at the same time?

> In your opinion, what should policy-makers, public service providers, corporations, educational institutions, and members of the civil society do to facilitate this family's settlement in Canada?

The Thomas Family

A family new to its present home

Wanda lives in a beautiful home on Bear Cove, a rural coastal community in Austin County, Nova Scotia. She resides with her husband, Jason, and her four wonderful children, sons Davis, aged four, Donald, aged three, and her daughters Cassie, aged two, and step-daughter Olive, aged eighteen. Wanda is what one considers a "Come From Away'er" (a person who moved into the area); she was born and raised in British Columbia and considers Langley home. Growing up, Jason had a very dysfunctional relationship with his family, so he wanted to return to his home town of Bear Cove in an effort to reconnect with his family.

After the birth of the couple's first child, he asked Wanda if she would consider moving to the Austin County area. In 2005, after their second child, the family purchased one of the area's prestigious homes, and moved into it one year later in 2006, after the birth of their third child. Wanda chose to remain in British Columbia until after delivery to ensure she had adequate medical service in the event there were complications with her third pregnancy. She knew that the Austin General Hospital did not have the services of an obstetrician or a maternity unit and because of the Province's doctor shortages, it was almost impossible to acquire the medical services of a general practitioner.

The move to Bear Cove separated Wanda from her entire support network of family and friends. She comes from a blended family with two older sisters from her dad's first marriage and a step-brother and half-sister from his second union. Wanda's step-mother calls every day at 1:00 Eastern time except when her daughter is visiting. "I have an overbearing, controlling step-mother; here I can do what I want." Wanda missed her family and best friend very much; they were close and got together for visits every two weeks. "I have no family here and it is very hard; I feel so alone and so isolated." Unfortunately, Jason was not able to rekindle the spirit of unity with his own family in the Austin County area.

Wanda has met what she considers lots of girlfriends in Austin; however she feels that they shut her out and do not invite her into their circle of friends and family. These women have their own little cliques and are in their own worlds with their mothers, sisters, grandmothers, and cousins. They only include Wanda when they have home-based or cottage-industry parties (candle/scrap booking parties), expecting her to show up with her wallet and purchase items to increase their sales and commissions. Wanda has met three friends in Austin whom she feels comfortable with and accepted by. These women are not from the Austin area; they too are "come from Away'ers" and have relocated to the area.

When Wanda moved to the area, she registered her children for play groups and hoped this would give her an opportunity to socialize with other women. She was welcomed and felt comfortable at the Austin County Family Resource Centre and the Austin county Library. However, when Wanda attended the play group in her own community in Bear Cove she was treated with the utmost disrespect from the other women present. They ignored Wanda and would not talk to her or include her in the group. This is the general treatment Wanda received from many in the community. She believed they were shunning her because she was not from the area. Wanda said, "You would swear I had pimples on the end of my nose and [was] diseased."

Wanda and Jason are experiencing challenging times due to mold and structural damage to their home, defects concealed by the previous home owners at the time of purchase. These individuals are prominent members of the community and Wanda fears that the dispute with these families will cause problems for her son when he starts school, and for the family in general.

Wanda is a recovering alcoholic and drug addict and has to be careful of her emotions. Her mind can play tricks on her. She does not attend Alcoholics Anonymous (AA) as regularly as she used to because of Jason's work schedule, and the cost of baby sitters for the children. Wanda believes she has to remember where she comes from and talk about her addictions.

"Going to AA reminds me who I am. I am a raging alcoholic. I remind myself if I drink or got a rock of cocaine my children wouldn't matter." Wanda continuously reminds herself of this so that she does not easily relapse. Wanda's biological mother was an alcoholic, her dad is a recovering alcoholic, and her husband Jason is a recovering alcoholic and drug addict. Wanda's children, husband, and faith in God keep her strong and determined to stay clean.

Lack of employment in the area has forced Jason to relocate to Saskatoon for work. Wanda is now alone in Austin County, with no family support and no husband. Recently, Wanda became emotionally overloaded with life's issues and she had what she described as a "breakdown." Wanda did not share these feelings with anyone. She explained, "I want everybody to think I'm okay out here...It's hard to reach out when you're in that state and crying." Wanda did not feel sorry for herself, but instead she felt lost.

Wanda is determined to be the best mother possible and not expose her children to the life of pain and abuse she experienced as a child. Like all mothers she wants the best for children. Wanda spends time listening, teaching, guiding, protecting and loving her children. She expects her children will live with peace and honesty, that they are trustworthy, loving, giving and content with themselves and who they are: "when they lay their heads down on their pillow at night, ... they know they did their best that day."

Discussion Questions:

> Why do you think Wanda has not managed to make friends in her new community?
> Is there something she could do, in addition to what she is already doing, to make herself feel more 'at home' in Bear Cove?
> What kind of public services is Wanda most likely to benefit from?

The Casp Family

A family living in poverty

Julia grew up in a Canadian military family with her parents, brother, and sister. Her family lived in Europe for a short time, as well as in Calgary briefly. She spent most of her youth in the Maritimes where she met the future father of two of her children. Currently she resides in Calgary, and is living in Regional Housing. She is a single mom supporting three children, receives social assistance (Supports for Independence, called SFI) and has assistance in her home from a family support worker.

Julia met the father of her two eldest children while she was seventeen and in high school. Rick was a few years older and had been to jail a number of times. Soon she fell in love and a short while later found out that she was pregnant This knowledge did not stop the abuse that Rick had been using against Julia since early on in their relationship over issues such as money or their relationship. At first the abuse was "more mental than anything else", but over time, the interactions got increasingly violent, to the point where Julia had to involve the police. One particular incident was so violent that she was "sure [her] life was over".

Julia tried to finish her high school diploma, but Rick decided to move to Manitoba with his family, which would allow him to escape the warrant that was out for his arrest. Julia followed him only to return to her family and friends when the abuse got to be too much. Her feelings were strong: "How am I going to stay away from him?... I was still attached to him." Julia had come from a childhood where her "dad was abusive as well...and so to be in the same type of relationship was just comfortable". After some time, feeling distant from him and being manipulated and coerced back to him, she joined Rick in Ontario briefly, but again returned to the Maritimes and her family.

Her son John was born surrounded by family and friends. Rick had surprisingly shown up the day before the due date, to be there and "make sure his son was given his last name". Although Rick was in his son's life for his first three weeks, he went to jail after Julia's mother called "the cops on him" after she saw her daughter being punched in the face with the baby in the room. With Rick in jail, Julia moved out on her own with her son John, although Rick returned many times over a year and a half. When the abuse against herself, her friends, and lastly her son got to be too much, Julia moved with her family to Calgary, where Julia lived with her parents or her brother and worked on and off. Within a short time, Rick arrived in Calgary to try and get back together with Julia. Julia was not interested in having Rick back in her life, but it was hard to remain separate from the father of her son. For Rick, "wherever John is, I am going to be". Julia allowed Rick to "break the restraining order so he could see his son". She intended to keep her relationship strictly platonic, based purely on the fact that Rick was the father of her son, but once Julia and Rick spent a night together, and their second child, Abby, was conceived.

Now Julia was pregnant, alone, and with low self esteem. She had "put a lot on hold for [Rick]" and she hadn't done "anything with [her] life, [she] had let [herself] go". She acknowledged that the "way [she] was parenting was really affecting...the way that John was being brought up". She had Abby while living at her parents' house. Rick denied that the child was his, even though Julia, who had attachment issues and fear about being in any sort of physical relationship, had not been with anyone else. Not long after the birth of Abby Julia made a commitment to go back to school. She was accepted into a Business Administration Program at the Southern Alberta Institute of Technology (SAIT). The program was paid for, as she was on Maternity Employment Insurance (EI). A few weeks into her program, she got a call from Regional Housing, informing her that she qualified for low income housing. Never having lived on her own in Calgary, Julia accessed the Salvation Army in order to furnish her new home. Julia was "overwhelmed" and found herself depending increasingly on the friendship of Dave, someone she had known from the Maritimes.

Julia and Dave starting seeing each

other often, and Julia found herself either "in love, obsessed, or compulsive" with him. Eventually Julia was pregnant with her third child, Rachel. Julia and Dave struggled to define their relationship. Although initially Dave outwardly expressed support, he also expressed loyalties he had to his children from a previous relationship. Over time he distanced himself until eventually he was out of the relationship, leaving Julia and her soon-to-be three children on their own. Julia, with the pressure of having to pay her $30,000 tuition loan if she failed or dropped out, finished her certificate program at SAIT.

The few months after her graduation and before her third child were a struggle because Julia was unable to find work because of her pregnancy and she could not get EI because she had just finished school. She contacted Children Services, so she could get the support of a Family Support Worker, as well as SFI. With every step Julia was making forward, she felt like "there was always ten walls that I had to climb to get to the achievement that I'm always supposed to have". She started attending programs at Catholic Social Services (CSS). She was confident and told Dave at the hospital when she had her baby, "Do you not realize that I will find a way to make this work!" Julia has remained committed to the program at CSS.

There she has learnt that, "I had to build my own self-esteem". She started watching her weight and increasing her positive self image and is "acknowledging all the things that [she] has done for [her] kids.... ." She has been working on her mental health and is seeing a counselor to deal with the family violence in her past. She continues to work with a Family Support Worker, receives SFI, and accesses the food bank when she needs to.

Julia recognizes the connection with her "past and how it all reflects into [her] present right now". The changes in her mental health and her family's increased stability have also resulted in positive changes for the children. Early on John had speech delays, especially after witnessing violence against his mother. Both he and Abby took part in Early Education classes. At home Julia had let her kids "run wild and free, for a lack of a better word". For Abby and John alike, as they were growing up, they "never knew what to do; they were unsure, they were always afraid they were going to get smacked, or they were going to get yelled at". Today, things have changed. Julia has learnt about the importance of consistency in her parenting, although she has to work really hard, and stop herself often. She has started to work on "decreasing the yelling, and increasing the talking".

Also, Julia is spending more time with her family. The first activity they started doing together was the family walk. Initially Julia had to make a point of setting a time for the whole family to go out for a walk, but now they are asking her to go.

Julia realizes "We've had a lot of downfalls, and we've had a lot of hardships, but… that's done now and this is what we've got to look forward to". Julia wants a bright future for her children, for them to know even though there are "some things in your life that you can't control, you can still do something about it to fix it". For Julia success means "to achieve something that you didn't think was achievable".

She wants to support her children in their reading, speech, and writing, and to introduce Rachel to books and stories. Something Julia learnt at her course at CSS sums up how she currently sees her family: "The family as a whole, and how to interact with them in everything you do, instead of you know, get away from me, and don't help me with this…and now… you are interacting with them, and you're having fun with them. I am so proud when we are all together and…everyone's getting along, and we're all quiet and we are teaching [Rachel] things, and just hearing them laugh…I'm proud".

Discussion Questions

> Julia has overcome many obstacles and has actively sought help from several different places. How important do you think it is for different service providers to work together with a family?
> If Julia and her family came to you seeking assistance, how would you support her?
> Julia had come from a childhood where her "dad was abusive as well…and so to be in the same type of relationship was just comfortable." What is your reaction to this statement?

The De Sousa Family

A family living in poverty

Lisa is a forty-year-old single mother with a two-year-old daughter named Sofia. They live in a two-bedroom apartment located in the downtown area of the city. Lisa's parents and brother live in a different city and she rarely sees them. She feels that she gets limited support from her family and she does not have many friends around.

She was never married to Sofia's father. She describes him as abusive, alcoholic, and a drug user. "He threatened my life and her life when I was still carrying her and I had to have him arrested." She explains that she would not like her daughter to meet him at this point because he could have a bad impact on her life. She is open to future involvement, though, if he "gets tested and proves that Sofia is his child." But at present Lisa has no contact with him or his family. She says that she is really sad to see her daughter grow up without a father but that she has a grandfather and uncle who love her, even if she doesn't see them very often.

Lisa suffers from fibromyalgia, chronic fatigue, polycystic ovarian syndrome and Type 2 diabetes. She has been prescribed a lot of medications to address her sleeping troubles, relieve her body pain and assist with her bouts of depression. However, she refuses to take any of the medications because she feels that medicine will damage her body and when she gets older, the medicine will no longer have any effect on her. She is also scared of the side effects the medicine may have.

Lisa is not happy with the health service in her city. She is currently on a disability support program. She has visited many doctors over the years.

She says that most of them "are cranky, overworked, and overloaded…" She describes her visits to the doctor as being "short, not personal, and careless." On the other hand, she really likes her daughter's pediatrician. "She is really nice…very helpful…and very gentle…."

Because of her illnesses, Lisa is very careful with the food she eats. She doesn't get any food from food banks in her community because, she says, the food that they give away contains chemicals and sugar. She cooks all the meals she and her daughter eat. She prefers to cook with organic vegetables but because of her economic situation she says that it is hard to keep a healthy diet. "I cook all the meals for my daughter and as a result I think she is one of the healthiest children I've seen."

Lisa has been on her disability subsidy for about ten years. She thinks that it is unfair that because of her illnesses, she and her daughter have to live in "sub-human conditions" and in poverty. "I have been unfortunate enough to be sick" she comments. She would love to go back to work but she says her body is not strong enough yet. She feels exhausted some days and says that it is hard for her to even keep up with the house-work.

Lisa describes her community as nice and safe. However, she says that because many gay people live in her neighborhood, she finds it very difficult to find a partner "I am heterosexual in a gay community so I don't meet a lot of people." She sometimes feels discriminated against by people in the neighborhood; " Believe it or not, they treat me like they're prejudiced against me because I am not gay."

Lisa does not take public transit. She says that she cannot afford it. Therefore, she walks everywhere and sometimes that makes it difficult for her to go to places outside her community. She is happy to have all she needs close to her house ,such as a grocery store, the doctor's office, hospitals, children's programs, *etc.*

She would love to take her daughter to nice places outside the city. She explains, "I would love to go to the zoo…[but] it's crazy expensive". She explains that she might be able to pay for public transit one way to a place but that she would have to walk back —and this makes the zoo impossible.

She attends different children's programs in her community and she describes them as useful for her daughter's learning and play. She meets a lot of people but feels that there is a language barrier: "I find that in this neighborhood there's [many] cultures and it's sometimes quite the barrier."

Lisa's daughter has recently started daycare. Sofia is eligible for a full childcare subsidy. She is attending two days a week and is currently on the waiting list to attend full time. Before being able to take Sophia to daycare, Lisa says she would spend the day taking care of her daughter all by herself; for two full years they were never apart. She says that sometimes she felt overwhelmed and tired. "I've actually lost my temper with her and I yelled at her a couple of times and it was because I was so exhausted."

When Sofia is not in daycare Lisa attends different drop-in programs with her, which she finds very useful for them both. She explains that she likes to talk to other adults and that she gets support from people running the programs. She says that she would like to have some free children programs during the weekends as well. She explains that sometimes she would like to go out at night or late in the afternoon and there are no programs that will take care of her daughter at those times or on the weekend. Lisa feels refreshed and happier to see her daughter going to daycare. She actually misses her daughter but she feels that she could be a better parent if she has a rest. "It has only been two days and I'm a different person, I'm happier, I feel like I can think straight and I'm interacting more with adults, which feels better…"

Lisa would like to find a person who will love her and her daughter. She dreams of having a house: "It doesn't have to be a big house; it can be a tiny house with a little backyard." She would like to be out of poverty and as healthy as possible. She expects her daughter to be happy and healthy.

Discussion Questions:

> What is your initial reaction to Lisa's story?
> Lisa faces many health challenges and has not had positive experiences with the health care system. What would you do to help her overcome the barriers that she faces?
> Sofia's attendance at daycare has helped Lisa. "It has only been two days and I'm a different person, I'm happier, I feel like I can think straight and I'm interacting more with adults, which feels better…." What suggestions could you make to further support Lisa and Sofia?
> Poverty places many stressors on families. List all the stressors that you think poverty may cause. What could you do to address these stressors?

The Levi Family

A family living in poverty

Rebecca Levi is a thirty-four-year-old Caucasian female who grew up in the Maritimes with a sister, brother, and both her parents. Her father continues to live in the Maritimes though Rebecca moved to British Columbia when she was twenty-five years old. She married Jacob six years ago and they have a daughter who is five years old, and two sons, aged three, and ten months.

Rebecca says she grew up in modest household in which both her parents had good jobs with benefits. She does not recall having excess, but remembers always having food and the bills were paid. Rebecca says her memories of childhood are positive and sees her upbringing as contributing to her current values and morals. She experienced a significant loss when her mother recently died from cancer. She was emotionally close to her mother and misses her all the time.

Rebecca did not experience poverty until after she was married and gave birth to her first child. She resigned from her job after having a baby. It was not affordable to pay for child care and return to work so Rebecca stayed at home to focus on being a mother and raising her children. Poverty has impacted Rebecca in practical ways, such as needing to go to the food bank. It has also had an emotional impact, because she now feels like outside forces control her life such as landlords and government agencies. She feels very vulnerable and ashamed asking for assistance, whether it be at the food bank or for a child care subsidy. She is unsure of the implications of accepting assistance. She is afraid that financial help can easily be taken away or taken back. She is untrusting of government involvement because she does not understand the complex system and has often experienced difficulty navigating the bureaucracy. Her attempts at is are difficult because when she phones for information, she is unable to remain on hold with government services because she has three children under five to care for. Her husband makes a good wage but must contribute 30% of his 'before tax' pay to family maintenance to support a child from a previous relationship. The amount of money remaining is not sufficient to support his wife and their three children. Rebecca and Jacob both accept that child support must be paid, but they do not understand how to cope with their particular circumstance. The end result is a family of five living in poverty, able to pay only most of their day-to-day living bills but always with insufficient money left over for food at the end of the month.

As Rebecca says, "We don't want (to) live high on the hog; ...we just want to live." Rebecca is sad she must move and leave her friends. She feels she has no choice. Jacob has struggled with addiction issues, which have contributed to the family's financial and emotional insecurity. Rebecca has experienced two episodes of post-partum depression with the most serious after the birth of her second child. At this time, she was hospitalized and this was a frightening time for Rebecca because she needed help but also needed to care for her children. She had no personal or support network to speak of and she felt alone and afraid. Rebecca has essentially functioned as a single parent for most of the past five years because her husband works in another province and comes home for only short stays.

Rebecca has remained optimistic despite her struggles with depression, poverty, her husband's addiction, and the death of her mother. She finds great peace in her spiritual beliefs and attributes her positive attitude to her belief that despite all obstacles, her inner strength anchors her, and she believes she can handle anything that comes her way. She admits she gets down but she is quick to point out that she never gives up.

Rebecca sees the blessing in her need. If it had not been for her experience with poverty and depression, Rebecca does not know if she would have found the wonderful friends and supports that have carried her through. When she was hospitalized with depression, a whole new world opened up for her. Rebecca did not want to remain hospitalized and have her children placed in foster care. Her husband continued to work out of town and could not be there to support Rebecca. The hospital staff realized that Rebecca needed support and referred her to a program that provided a mentor who would visit in her home and offer an ear to listen and some practical support when possible. What happened next has led to nothing short of transformative for Rebecca. She felt vulnerable and alone with her children in a city that was not home for her. She had no close confidants and very little money. Rebecca began a process of connection that resulted in a network of both formal and informal supports that have allowed her to develop friendships and resources that meet her emotional and social needs in addition to some practical support such as babysitting.

Rebecca hopes that that all parents have the opportunity to develop supports as she did. She says they were essential for her well-being. She worries that some people are too isolated and have no way to hear about different programs that are free. Rebecca would like to see a network of information made available in coffee shops and on public notice boards for those people who have no Internet or who don't know where to look for the information. She thinks she is one of the lucky ones who found one person to start the ball rolling. She does not know what would have happened if she did not get help at the hospital.

Over the course of a few years, she has become a woman with a weekly routine incorporating several family programs aimed at offering child development opportunities, parent education and support, and socialization with other moms. Most important is the opportunity to connect with women who "do not judge", whom Rebecca now calls friends. Her children have opportunities to grow and develop as individuals with a structured routine, turn taking, and opportunities for following rules, which is very important to Rebecca. She wants her children to know right from wrong and to learn how to socialize with other children.

Rebecca wishes she had more opportunity to register her children in organized sports to help teach them teamwork and leadership skills but that is unaffordable for her and there does not seem to be financial support for that type of activity. As well, she finds it difficult to manage a schedule that is too rigid, given the sometimes unpredictable needs of her three children. She would like to see the availability of drop-in soccer or baseball programs offered the same way as drop-in play groups she currently attends. Rebecca identifies that her lack of money is not her only obstacle when it comes to establishing some 'adult only' activities. She sees her own issues with trust as preventing her from having a more formalized support network that could allow her breaks from her parenting in order to pursue some of her interests such as employment as a veterinary assistant. Rebecca has difficulty leaving her children with others because she has been the only one to take care of them and does not know anyone well enough to trust them with her children. Poverty has contributed to several moves for this family, which in turn leaves Rebecca with no long-term relationships built on trust.

Rebecca sees her job as a mother to take on the role of 'teacher' whenever possible. She says "I want to be able to give them something, and then get something more from an ECE educator or somebody else besides myself." She views her job as laying the foundation, providing the "building blocks". In addition to having the skills to prepare them for life, Rebecca wants her children to "be good to everybody" to know that "we are all treated equal." As well, she wants them to have family traditions; if she saw her children develop this in their lives, she feels they would have success. Rebecca wants her children to know the value of teamwork because "If you are a team you can accomplish anything."

Discussion Questions:

> Rebecca says that she had a positive childhood. How do you think this experience helps her cope with her present situation?
> Because she has had to seek assistance, Rebecca feels she has lost control of her life and is vulnerable. How would you address this concern?
> How would you change your service to better meet Rebecca's needs?

The Mackensie Family

A family living in poverty

Maggie Mackensie is a single mother raising three children, all under the age of five. Despite having to endure many challenges and overcome obstacles, Maggie maintains a positive attitude and believes that her life and her children's lives will get better. Currently, Maggie and her three children live in an apartment but she believes that one day they will live in a house with a nice back garden where the children can play. It is this positive outlook that gets Maggie through the days when she feels overwhelmed with her situation.

Maggie is certainly no stranger to facing hard times. She was born and raised in the same small coastal town where she lives today. She had a difficult childhood as she and her two brothers were raised in a home with an alcoholic father and a mother who did not spend time with her children or in doing "typical mother - daughter activities" with Maggie. She was rarely home and when she was, most of the time was spent arguing with her husband, leaving the responsibility for the younger brothers on Maggie's shoulders. Maggie's parents eventually separated because of her mother having an affair, and the little bit of family life they did have fell apart. To this day, Maggie has a very difficult time trusting her parents and does not confide in them as many children do with their parents. She still does not forgive them for the life she had growing up. Maggie remembers a lot of fighting in the home during her childhood, which made it very difficult for her to complete her school work or even concentrate while in school. Nevertheless, she did manage to graduate from high school successfully, despite the lack of parental support.

It was during high school that Maggie formed a serious relationship with a young man she had known most of her life. Once she graduated, she moved to Ontario with him to find work but they didn't stay long and soon moved back to their home town, where they lived together for twelve years. Maggie and David have three children together; Darlene is now four and will start kindergarten soon, Roger is two, and Justin is four months. Maggie and David recently separated because Maggie simply could not handle David's lack of support as a partner and as a father. David began dabbling in drugs, spending night after night away from home, and coming home late at night, while Maggie was left at home to care for three small children. Having grown up with an alcoholic father, she could not imagine putting her own children through what she had endured. "I grew up with an alcoholic …I had that growing up; I didn't want it anymore. You just get tired of the same old routine. I don't want my kids to go through it." When her youngest was hospitalized for pneumonia and she found herself handling it completely on her own, she had had all she could take and the couple ended their relationship.

Maggie found life without David a huge adjustment. Even though David was not around a lot at the end of their relationship, she still had a lot of good memories of their years together and is very hurt at the way it ended and their lack of communication. The children miss him greatly. Her oldest child Darlene has a hard time dealing with the fact that her daddy is no longer living in their home. It makes it even harder for them to know that he is now living with another woman who also has young children. There is no set visitation schedule in place. David calls for one or all three of the children whenever "he feels like it" and he doesn't spend as much time with them as he should. When Darlene does visit her father, she becomes very confused and resentful.

David offers Maggie no financial support. When they were together, there was never enough money to make ends meet and they lived "from check to check". Maggie worked in the beginning but after having three children so close together and experiencing health problems, she found it impossible to find a job. David would work odd jobs with little pay, but the family was also subsidized through social assistance. There is very little money for any extras and Maggie also has to contend with paying off bills that she and David once shared together. She feels like she should be the one supporting her children but admits that there are benefits for her right now to being on the system. The children attend child care programs, which is covered by social assistance.

Maggie also has to contend with her middle child's medical condition. Roger has been diagnosed with a rare genetic condition, which affects his hair, nails, weight, teeth, and skin. He suffers from extremely bad eczema, has sensitivity to certain foods, and does not have sweat glands, which causes extreme discomfort and irritability. Roger has already made several trips to the hospital to see special doctors and there will undoubtedly be more visits to make in the future. Thankfully, social assistance helps with the costs of these medical trips. Learning her son had this condition was not the only upset for Maggie. Genetic testing led her to discover the man she had known all her life as her dad was not her biological father. Her real father lives in the same community and Maggie and her children are working on building a relationship with him now. Maggie has two sisters whom she knew nothing about until recently but she claims the man who raised her will always be her dad and it doesn't change the way she feels about him. She was more upset by the fact that she does not share the same father with her two brothers. It has not affected her relationship with her brothers though; in fact, it seems to have brought them closer.

Right now, Maggie is excited about Darlene starting school and is proud of how bright her little girl is. She attended the Kinderstart program at school where she thrived and is ecstatic about starting school. Maggie is hoping that Darlene will receive some counseling from a family therapist or child psychologist in the near future to help her deal with the recent changes in her life since her dad left. Maggie's social worker is helping to make the arrangements. She takes her children to the local playground when she can; it is over a mile away and they have to walk there. Not having a car limits the family in the things they can do. The nearest swimming pool, bowling alley, or shopping mall is an hour's drive away and Maggie admits it's harder in the summer time because you need a car just to be able to take your children to a beach. Her children love to play outside near their apartment building and Maggie does what she can to engage them in creative and educational activities in the home, like reading and doing crafts together. She is planning on attending the parent-children programs at the Family Resource Center in the fall. Maggie has a great friend/neighbour who is also a single mother with three children so they are able to offer support to each other. She does not have much of a social life or any social opportunities for herself but says, "That's okay because right now my life is my kids and I put all my energy into making their lives the best they can be."

Maggie does not have a good relationship with her own mother but acknowledges that her mother is trying harder with her grandchildren than she did with her own children. Maggie is trying to trust her. The children spend time with David's mother in a nearby community and Maggie hopes their relationship will continue to grow. Maggie hopes Darlene and her two boys will grow up to be responsible, respectful, smart, and able to make their own choices. She hopes to move away from their home town someday so she can go to school to learn a trade and find a good job to support her children. Maggie has many talents and passions; she can draw, paint, sew, make clothes, do wood working, and cut hair. As a teenager she dreamed of a career as a gourmet chef or an interior decorator. One day she will put her skills to good use and earn a living for her family doing what she loves. When asked what she hopes life will be in ten years, Maggie sums it up by saying, "I hope it's a lot better than what it has been the last ten years. Hopefully I get a good, stable job, or go back to school and get a good job for me and my kids. Now that I'm a single mom, it's going to be a lot harder but I've been through worse."

Discussion Questions:

> Imagine that you have just met Maggie and heard her story. What would you say to her?
> Maggie is working with a range of different professionals, such as a social worker, a kindergarten teacher, and medical specialists. Suggest ways that these professionals can collaborate in order to better meet Maggie's needs.
> What do you think Maggie's life might look like in ten years' time?

The Malter Family

A family living in poverty

Yvette Malter was born in August of 1971 into a life of poverty. She is the youngest of five children raised by a single mom. As a child, Yvette's mother was a resident of a Home for Colored Children for several years, until being rescued by family members and removed from the orphanage in her late teens. Yvette describes her mother as low-functioning intellectually, though credits her for "doing the best with what she had." Several of Yvette's sibling experienced mental illnesses and traumas for which they never received counseling, support, or treatment. Yvette's eldest sister was a victim of incest beginning at age thirteen at the hands of an adult uncle with whom she lived in a long-term abusive and torturous relationship (twenty-three years). Yvette's eldest brother had schizophrenia and her other sister was raised in foster care in a neighboring county. Growing up, Yvette had to struggle in silence to make sense of the world around her because "no one would discuss anything that was going on."

Yvette is an African Canadian woman residing in a rural fishing community. She shares a small two-bedroom apartment in the downtown core with her sons Josh, aged eighteen, and Ron, aged fifteen. Yvonne's three-year-old son, Brian, lives with his father twenty kilometers away. Her painful decision to relinquish custody of her son was a result of harassing and threatening behavior by Brian's father. His threats included filing neglect and abuse complaints with Family and Children Services. Though his allegations were false, Yvette chose not to challenge these threats based on her negative childhood experiences with the Department of Community

Services (DCS) and Family and Children Services. Yvette reluctantly submitted to the demands and gave her son away. While she remains in the child's life, visits are irregular and controlled by Brian's father. Yvette preferred not talk about Brian and became distraught and withdrawn when asked to discuss the child.

At the age of nineteen, having completed a grade ten education, Yvette left school when she became pregnant with her first child. After the birth of Josh, Yvette was in receipt of Family Benefits from DCS. She moved to the city to be close to family for support in raising her new baby. Two years later she became pregnant with Ron. Wanting to "find herself" Yvette moved back to the fishing community.

Now on her own, and without family support Yvette found things very difficult. Six months into her second pregnancy while cooking breakfast for Josh, Yvonne had her hydro disconnected. She begged the technician to "please wait until I finish cooking the eggs." He denied her request. She was without hydro for one month. Yvette had to go to a friend's house to bathe. Once Ron was born the family moved back to the city. Yvette says "I felt like a gypsy."

A couple of years later Yvette once again moved her family back to the small fishing community. When Ron

started school, Yvette gained employment at a local grocery store. After working several odd jobs, she ended back on Family Benefits with the DCS. At this time she was forced to take a sixteen-week skills development and job readiness program sponsored by DCS, called "WINGS". If she did not attend the program, her Family Benefits would be discontinued. Yvette was not paid for child care or transportation and she felt degraded and humiliated. Yvette organized a protest to challenge the agency's practices. The television media reported on the protest and several organizations provided support to Yvette and the other women. Yvette said that this resulted in "us women" meeting with the DCS managers and several issues such as the cost of child care and transportation were resolved. Also, the program's curriculum was changed to reflect adult content. "DCS thought they were dealing with dummies, I was not a dummy.... We got good and bad feedback after the protest: ...Myself, if I need something, they would give it to me to shut me up."

At age six Ron was diagnosed with Oppositional Defiance Disorder. The doctor told Yvette about this personality disorder, but no treatment or support was made available. Fortunately, Ron's school principal worked closely with the family to support him. When the child was in grade six, a new principal was assigned to the school and Ron lost the only support he had. School became a place where Ron felt unwelcome. One day, Ron's teacher told him to stay inside at recess and complete his assignment. Defying her instruction Ron went out to play with his friends. As a result, the principal called the RCMP for assistance to manage the situation. Two RCMP officers from the local detachment arrived at the school, resulting in eleven-year-old Ron being embarrassed, scared, and belittled. His love of learning diminished after this incident.

"Josh will complete his education in an adult school. He is currently eighteen in grade ten. The average age for Black males to graduate in my community is 20 years of age....There is a change in racism since I was in school. Things are worse. I see racism more in the school with my sons than with me."

Yvette finds it very challenging raising Black males because of the racist climate and discriminatory practices. She is confronted with the reality that her sons will be denied equal access to education and employment. The expectations Yvette has for her sons is that they graduate and get good paying jobs. But she is convinced that the family will have to move away from the small community for these things to happen. "Perhaps to a larger city like Toronto where there are many nationalities and my boys can just blend in."

Discussion Questions:

> Yvette feels that racism has worsened since she was in school. How would you approach this concern when talking with Yvette and with other families that you work with?

> At age six, Ron was diagnosed with Oppositional Defiance Disorder. Because this condition was not fully understood by his teachers, Ron had trouble at school. What measures could be taken to ensure Ron has a positive school experience?

> Living in poverty often results in feelings of inadequacy and humiliation. What can be done to change this?

The Millwood Family

A family living in poverty

Dawna Millwood is a white Canadian female who was born in the late sixties and is an only child. Her parents married when her mother became pregnant, but the relationship did not last as her father was abusive. Though baptized Catholic, Dawna prefers to think of herself as spiritual rather than religious.

Growing up, she felt isolated and lonely. Her mother abused her emotionally and eroded her self-esteem by saying that she wished that Dawna had been a boy, and by constantly criticizing her, and saying things like, "Oh, you are just like your father." At times her mother used physical abuse such as shaking and hitting. She often went to bed hungry, not because they did not have money but because her mother did not take care of her. According to Dawna, her mother was very social and articulate, had a car and was always well-dressed and well-groomed so outsiders did not suspect negligence or abuse. She believed that keeping up appearances was very important to her mother.

In school, Dawna would steal other students' lunch from their boxes and gulp it down while hiding in the cloakroom. She feels she has issues about weight and was anorexic because of this. She also equates food with being rich. She said that when she went to her father's house when she was nine, she realized he was "rich", not because of his house or car, but because his fridge was full of food.

In grade two, she was identified as having dyslexia, so she did not start reading until she was nine years old. Today she loves to read, buys many books, and describes herself as "well read".

When Dawna was a young teenager, she and her mother lived in a Co-Op building. There she met interesting and creative people who provided an antidote to her mother's emotionally abusive attitude. A troupe of Cirque de Soleil-type clowns taught her to juggle and invited Dawna to go with them for the summers to work at a camp in California. Her mother allowed it, happy to have her gone, Dawn believes. Dawna loved these adventures away from her mother and enjoyed living within the "family" of performers. The one positive lesson she learned from her mom was to always be clean, presentable, and neat.

After high school, Dawna left home to go it alone. She made a living by taking seasonal work such as picking fruit and tree planting in rural Canada. When she was twenty-three, she became pregnant with her first son, Sam. The father was a casual farm worker and she does not have any contact with him. She went on social assistance when Sam was born. Sometimes she worked part time, taking money under the table so that her social assistance cheque would not decrease. After a short time she and Sam moved back to the city because she felt isolated in the small town because she felt, "There was a real stigma toward single moms on welfare".

At this time she was accepted into a nursing program, but she became pregnant again so she dropped out in her first semester. Her second son, Mikey, was born in 1993. His father was an engineering student and he wanted her to have an abortion. They broke up when she refused to do so. During the next six years, she drifted across Canada with her two boys, living only on social assistance. She lived in 19 different places, moving each time she fell behind in the rent. She liked to "treat" her sons with trips and interesting experiences rather than paying rent: "I thought I could be both a free-spirit and a mother".

Mikey's father finally reported her to Children's Aid Society (CAS), claiming she was an incompetent and unstable mother. Both her sons were apprehended — although the children were well adjusted, clean, and well fed, the facts of her nineteen addresses in four provinces in the previous six years, and of not having enrolled the boys in school were seen as neglect; she was declared to be "unstable and a flight risk". She lost custody of her two boys and was ordered by the court to attend parenting classes and undergo psychological testing. However, she was allowed supervised access to the children because there were no signs of abuse. Currently, Sam, now fourteen, lives with a foster family, and Mikey, twelve, lives with his father and step-mother.

Dawna recently had a third son, Paul, who is twenty-two months old. His father does not live with them, but offers financial and emotional support. She lives in a small rented apartment and relies on such assistance as the Child Tax Benefit and GST, to which she is entitled as she has zero income. Over the years, she has lived in council housing, gone to food banks, and taken welfare cheques, but currently she is managing to make ends meet. She is very aware of the stigma of being poor and she worries about what people will think of her. "I always worry that if he [Paul] cries, people will think I'm a bad mother."

Dawna wants success and status for her sons but she also wants them to have friends and be well thought of. "An 'A' grade means nothing if you are not a good and thoughtful person".

Discussion Questions:

> How have Dawna's experiences had an impact on her attitudes and values?
> What steps would you take to develop a trusting relationship with Dawna?
> What do service providers need to know about how poverty affects the lives of children and their families?

The Miyadunni Family

A family living in poverty

Jinder and his wife Shamila moved to Canada seven years ago from Sri Lanka. They came from different provinces in Sri Lanka and are of different religions, Jinder being of the Hindu faith and his wife being of the Islamic faith. This mixed marriage created a lot of stress between families, so the couple decided to move to Canada and raise their family here, thus relieving the stress on their families. Another reason for moving to Canada was to escape the political unrest in Sri Lanka. Jinder felt that since he was Tamil, he was not given an equal opportunity at education and employment there, where the Sinhalese were the dominant group in power.

Jinder states that he comes from a simple family with a strong cultural belief that families help each other out and parents sacrifice everything for their children. "Children respect and take care of their parents. Parents save money and land for their children. Parents do everything for their kids." He comes from an educated family; his mother and two sisters all have university degrees even though they remain at home to care for their children.

Moving to Canada was difficult because of the change of culture and lack of broad family support. Fortunately there was an uncle and his wife in Quebec who helped them find an apartment and facilitated their connection to the Tamil community. When their daughter was born a year after they arrived, they sought help from the Centre Local de Services Communautaires (CLSC), the government agency that provides health and social support in Quebec. Identified by the CLSC as a family in need of support, they were assisted by social workers to learn how to manage financially, where to shop, and how to economize.

When their second child, Vickram, a boy, was born two years later, everything was fine until his 18th month, when they noticed Vickram was no longer making eye contact or speaking. They immediately went to their physician and were counselled to wait and see. Jinder did not follow this advice, knowing that something was seriously wrong. He found the money to have a hearing test done privately for Vickram. As there was nothing wrong with his hearing, they were referred to the Autism Spectrum Disorder Clinic at Montreal's Children's Hospital. One year later, Vickram received a diagnosis of autism spectrum disorder.

Jinder and Shamila were devastated to watch their son's development regress. Vickram became very distracted and unfocused and was no longer the same little boy. They found a pre-school for children with special needs, which provided them with a subsidy, so he attended it three mornings each week. A year later, they received government support for twenty hours of therapy each week. These interventions helped Vickram, so he can now say a few words and sing along with familiar tunes. He is also more responsive than he was. In

September he will start school, integrated into a regular classroom.

Having a child with special needs had a major impact on this family. Jinder practices his Hindu religion and he would have liked his son to participate with him in their religious activities, but because Vickram could not sit still for prayers, he could not attend the temple. In Jinder's extended family, no one has autism or any intellectual challenges. Jinder didn't feel comfortable taking Vickram to meet his family in Sri Lanka. "I had never heard of autism before, and I didn't know what to do." Vickram could not go to child care because of his erratic behaviour, throwing toys, and constant movement. This created a lot of stress for Shamila. As she does not drive, she had to take Vickram on the bus to his pre-school. "It was very difficult, a big challenge," she said.

The challenges of a low-income immigrant family living in the Province of Quebec with a child with special needs are daunting. Jinder finds it impossible to learn French. His wife has managed to take the government-sponsored French language classes, but he has not been able to find the time to do this successfully. In spite of this obstacle, Jinder has been able to advocate for his family and especially for his son in order to obtain the help and services he requires. In Quebec, because of Bill

101, immigrant children must be educated in French, but Jinder was able to get an exemption for his son because he has special needs associated with learning disabilities. Now Jinder and Shamila will be better able to be involved in the education of their children, as it takes place in the English language with which they are both familiar.

Social workers advocated for them at first, enabling the family to learn how to navigate the systems in a new country, and get things in place for pre-school and primary school. A local community association provided financial subsidies to help them cover the adapted pre-school fees. This support, as well as the family's willingness to make sacrifices, has kept them optimistic despite their many challenges. "In my country, we do everything for the children. If we don't have the money, then we cut, cut, cut the things we need in order to buy for the children."

The family's social life consists of going to the temple to keep in contact with people of their culture. It is a welcoming place for people of all religions and their daughter is learning traditional dance and the Tamil language. Mr. and Mrs. Miyadunni hope their children will receive a good education so they will grow up to be independent and be able to take care of each other. They are concerned about their son but are optimistic because he is getting the services that he needs right now.

When asked how professionals can best serve them, Jinder replies that he respects everyone, no matter what colour, language, or education they have, so he expects the same from everyone with whom he comes in contact.

"Life is good! Daughter now [can] understand French, very proud of daughter. Son now [can] understand better and can even say his name, but says it with an English accent, not Tamil. Now Vickram is getting better, everything is good; we [are] happy!"

Discussion Questions:

> You have just met the Miyadunni family and listened to their story. Where and how would you begin to support this family?

> Jinder believes that "parents do everything for their kids." In what ways has the "system" assisted and/or hindered this family in their efforts to provide for their children?

> Identify the barriers that Jinder and his family face. What could you do to remove some of those barriers?

The Peter Family

A family living in poverty

A cat, a dog, two guinea pigs, an assortment of fish, and two preschool girls make up Anne's immediate family. They live in a two-story, rented, semi-detached home in a middle-class neighbourhood in a small urban centre in Ontario. This sole support, twenty-three-year-old mother parents Lauren, four, and Hailey, nine months old, on a full-time basis. Anne's familial support consists of her mother and boyfriend while the rest of her extended family lives two hours away.

Anne was born in a rural area and as a child lived in a variety of small and large urban centres. In 1998, at the age of fifteen, she moved to this small urban centre where, at the age of nineteen, she gave birth to Lauren, and to Hailey at the age of twenty-two. Recently, Anne moved from a duplex in a lower-income neighbourhood to her present home. Anne

made this decision and others so "at least my kids aren't growing up 'in the ghetto'". Her children "are out in a nice place with nice kids and schools and neighbours." Anne chose "to live in an expensive, beautiful place and have a little bit less money" because she views the public housing opportunities she qualifies for as "'disgusting'...I won't put my kids there".

Already at a financial disadvantage as a single parent who does not work outside the home, Anne realizes her decision to move to his new residence places her in an even more challenging financial position. When speaking about her economic status, Anne itemizes some difficult choices she has made so her children have this opportunity. They include omitting the true costs of her living expenses to 'her worker', going without dental care for herself, and working periodically for

158

cash only. "Food comes first and then bills are second – so I am behind on my phone bill… I am behind in my hydro bill…I pay the minimum every month… so they won't shut it off." Anne does not receive any financial support from Lauren and Hailey's father. "The money I do have is for food, diapers, formula, then bills, and then recreational stuff."

The benefits to being on social assistance for Anne's family include a free monthly bus pass because she attends the local Ontario Early Years Centres, dental care for the children, reimbursement for purchasing birth certificates for Hailey and Lauren, drug benefits, and the fact 'welfare' will not force her to work until Hailey is in school full-time. "I'm definitely grateful that I can stay home with my kids…I don't want day care raising my kids."

Social activities for Anne's family include attending the early years programs, playing in the park, McDonald's once a month, trips to Walmart, karate lessons for Lauren and, occasionally for Anne, going out to dinner with a male companion who pays for a sitter.

In the five years since Anne has had a family to take care of, she has had to work with a number of professionals to maintain the well-being of her family. Like any typical family with young children, the common practice of visiting doctors and dentists is also part of Anne's world. These visits take on a new dimension, however, for a young single parent. After the birth of Hailey, Anne recognized some signs and symptoms that she might be experiencing post-partum depression. "I [think] maybe it's just a bad month…maybe it's a bad three months…okay, it's been nine months now…and I'm still yelling…". Because Anne heard stories of other young mothers telling their doctors they were depressed and the doctors calling the Children's Aid Society (CAS), she was afraid to seek help, fearful she would have her children taken away. "So I refused to tell my doctor…they're going to call Children's Aid on me…so I'll just deal with it myself…."

Although Anne's previous contact with CAS was minimal (called because of a domestic dispute when Lauren was a baby), she still felt she needed to be careful.

Discussion Questions:

> How would you describe your role with this family?
> At one point in her narrative Anne states, "I don't want daycare raising my kids" and later she says she was afraid to seek help because she was fearful that Children's Aid would take her children away. What is your reaction to these comments?
> What would you identify as Anne's strengths?
> What steps would you take to build a relationship of trust and support for Anne and her family?

The Radley Family

A family living in poverty

Page Radley, a single parent suffering from depression and abuse from her son's father, is now renting a basement suite from her unsupportive mother for herself and her three-year-old son, Les, as she is not able to afford rent elsewhere. A thirty-year-old Canadian, Page grew up in Vancouver in a dysfunctional family; she wanted only love, affection, and support from her family, especially her mother. She found the perfect extended family from her first husband, which fulfilled all the needs she had vainly hoped to have filled by her own family. "They were... the family I never had".

Page suffered deeply after the break-up of that abusive first marriage and to get over it she found another partner. After a month of being together she got pregnant, at which time she found out about her new partner's abusive tendencies. She stayed with him in the hope he would change. After a year of being with him, she found a way out and went to her mother, who believes that Page should go back and 'fix things' with her son's father. "I still have family saying things like, 'You should be partners'."

Today Page's depression has not allowed her to work so she receives income assistance. She rents the downstairs of her mother's home as this is the only affordable housing she can find. However, this has not stopped her from working on herself or with her son. The benefits of being on income assistance are that everyday Page uses every free minute to 'play' with her son, read to him, and take him to various activities that promote healthy social, cognitive, and physical development. "I try to find activities for us to do where we are both needing to play a part in the play ... so it's not like here's a toy to like entertain you". And she feels lucky that she has this time to spend with her son. "I am hugely lucky in the fact that I...see that this is the opportunity to use...wisely with my child and for myself..."

Page also attends various activities for herself such as: parenting workshops, single parents support groups, Parent Educations Nights, and Counselling sessions to help her through her abusive relationship. She says, "One good thing coming out of this is that it affords me time to work on my depression and other problems." "You know I am a different person now because I had these services."

The main challenge on being on Income assistance is that every dollar counts. "it is hard to really budget yourself...even when I do really budget, there are lots of times where I just say, 'Wow, I am really down to my last dollar!' and there are lots of things that you just have to say no to ...I haven't had to use food banks.. I make sure I stay on top of things so that I save enough money..."

Page uses many of the free services that are offered in Vancouver. However, Page does feel that if there were more childminding services at the parenting workshops and Parent Education Nights, she would be able to attend them all. "Everyone I can get my hands on, I can access it".

For Les she says "I always hope that whatever school or anywhere that my son will be in his life, ...that he feels confident and safe to express,,, his feelings and that people in the environment he is in also reflect that back, and encourage and support [his] doing that."

Success for Page's son is being in an environment that he enjoys. For Page success has changed over the years. "Now it just means feeling comfortable with something that has happened or something you've achieved and that over all you've done your best...given your best."

Page's goals for the future are to raise a healthy child and to find a job that would provide her a humble home and to give back to the community what the community has given to her. Speaking of its services, she says, "Hopefully in the near future I won't need to access ones that always have to be free. But eventually I would like to give back those services whether it was donating time or money or lobbying for more services for single moms."

Page sees herself and Les in the future living a very simple life. "We would ...have a modest, comfortable, safe home of our own and some comfortable, modest, safe car. ... I don't see us ever having anything real elaborate but just like what ...serves our needs."

Discussion Questions:

> Page found herself in an abusive situation with the father of her son. What approaches would you take when working with someone who has suffered abuse?
> In what ways has receiving social assistance enabled Page to take care of herself and her son?
> Identify Page's strengths. How would you build on these strengths to further support her?

The Stevenson Family

A family living in poverty

Alyssa and her husband Brad live in a two bedroom, third-floor walk-up apartment in a rural township. They have two children, three-and-a-half-year-old Scott and seven-month-old Paula. Brad was in the military and is currently working straight nights at a factory. Alyssa has a DSW (Developmental Social Worker) diploma but currently works at a Tim Horton's mid afternoons until late evening.

Alyssa wants her children to have an easier life than she had. She believes the children need a good education in order to be successful. She defines this success as the ability to choose a job or profession they enjoy. In order to help her children achieve this, she and Brad save the "baby bonus" money for the children's post-secondary education. This is quite an accomplishment as the family has lim-

ited financial resources. It is a mark of her determination that her children have more opportunity than she had herself, that this money has been banked. Alyssa comes from a family where she is the only one with a college education and the only one with a job. She is proud of these accomplishments.

Her children's education is very important to her and she spends much of her time with them teaching them the skills she feels they need to learn. She is concerned that preschool programs are more concerned with fun and social development than they are with actual learning. She recently read a lot about the value of sign language for infants and has taught sign language to both children as she believes it is easier for the baby to communicate in this way. She is also teaching Scott to read and he already knows his alphabet, numbers and how to print his name. They are working on word recognition and simple addition. Alyssa is very proud of her children's accomplishments and is pleased that the pediatrician has labeled her children as advanced.

Alyssa believes that she needs to encourage teachers and other professionals to get to know her children through sharing information with them. She believes that professionals often think that parents are overreacting or that they don't put much value in the experiences of the parent. She feels that parents, especially moms, know their children better than anyone else and that their knowledge should be valued and utilized by the professionals that have an impact on their children.

Alyssa wants to have a home and a yard for her family. She believes that this goal may be met now that she has a job and they are able to put some money aside. She struggles daily with the difficulties of living in a three-floor walk up with a baby and a small child, a dog and two cats.

"The logistics for getting groceries is mind boggling as you have to have a stroller, a car seat for the taxi, your grocery bags and a diaper bag. The children can't be left alone and yet you have to transport everything to the apartment from the taxi".

Usually the family walks everywhere but grocery shopping is the one time they use a taxi. The lack of transportation for other services is a big concern for the family. They hope to eventually buy a car in order to lessen the difficulties experienced by living in a community with no public transportation system. Many services are located out of the area and the family will choose not to attend a program if it is not within reasonable walking distance from their apartment.

Alyssa does have family in a neighbouring community about a half hour drive away but does not visit very often as she has many conflicting emotions regarding many of her family members. She is close to a cousin who married her best friend and has found them to be good suppports to her. This is very important as Brad was away a great deal when he was in the military and Alyssa was very much a single parent for the first two and a half years of Scott's life. Brad has had to take on primary care for his children now that Alyssa is working and this has been a learning process for everyone. Alyssa is very organized and meticulous about her home and her children while Brad has a more relaxed attitude towards things. This has caused some friction but things are getting better.

Alyssa believes in contributing to her community and is currently teaching people in the neighbourhood to knit at the local resource centre. She is also involved in her church and hopes to create a clothing bank for families without the financial means to buy new. She wants to offer this service so that people do not have to prove need through administrative means and so they can maintain personal dignity and pride. She feels that if people want to exchange clothes or feel they need to get something they shouldn't have to prove it based on someone else's criteria.

Alyssa attends programs that are available locally whenever she can. She wants her children to socialize with others in their community. She also has enrolled Scott in preschool and is pleased that her new job has enabled this to continue. While she believes the program is too focused on fun she does realize that it plays an important role in Scott's social life, enabling him to develop friendships with others his own age. Scott has moved 14 times in his three and a half years and this has certainly had an effect on him. She would like to be able to enrol him in hockey but is discouraged as this is an expensive sport and most subsidies are not for working families.

Alyssa was a victim of domestic abuse in a past relationship and was stalked by her abuser even after Scott was born. This caused her to move frequently and to seek support through shelters and second stage housing in other communities She feels that this community where she now lives could benefit from facilities similar to those and believes that the fact there is nothing available in town is dangerous. Alyssa values trying to help others and has very definite ideas of how this help will be structured. Alyssa has a cousin who will soon be moving in with the family. Alyssa hopes to give the cousin the structure and stability that she believes is lacking in her cousin's life.

The family is hoping to move out of their apartment in May and get a house with the yard. This is important for Alyssa as Brad is working on rejoining the military and if successful this will once again necessitate a lot of travel and time away from his family.

Discussion Questions:

> Based on your own knowledge of families living in poverty, how does this story challenge your assumptions?

> Alyssa worries that "preschool programs are more concerned with fun and social development than they are with actual learning." What is your reaction to this statement, and what steps would you take to address this concern?

> Identify this family's strengths and discuss how you would encourage the family to build upon them.

> What role do parental values play in child-rearing?

APPENDIX II: INTERVIEW GUIDE

- Comment on the weather or make small talk about a non-controversial issue in the news to build rapport.
- Explain about the study.
- Explain the informed consent form and ask respondent to sign it.
- Request permission to audiotape interview.

I. Family Narrative

1. This research focuses on families and how professionals can better serve you and your children. Help me understand your story and what you expect of us.
   - Tell me about your family.
   - Tell me more about your child. How would you describe him/her?
2. What does it mean to your family to have a child with special needs/ to be newcomers in Canada/ to have limited income?
   - What are some of the challenges?
   - What are some of the benefits?
3. What support do you access as a parent?
   - You spoke about taking your child to the (FRP, park). What other things do you do with him/her?
   - What activities do you do for yourself?
   - What do you think about these activities/programs?
4. Which established agencies that you know of serve families in your neighbourhood ?
   - Which government or community agencies has your family used?
5. What changes would you propose to improve services and support for families like yours?

II. Expectations

6. What kind of expectations do you have of your child?
7. What do you think the child care/school's expectations are of your child?
8. What are your expectations of the school/child care/FRP for supporting the development/education of your child?
9. What things do you do with your child to support his/her development and learning?

10. What do you think are the school/child care/ FRP's expectations of you as a parent for educating your child?
    - Does their approach match your expectations for promoting your child's development/education?
11. How do you communicate with the teacher/early childhood educator to support your child's development/learning?
12. How would you like professionals to communicate and collaborate with you to achieve success for your child?
    - What can professionals do to gain your trust?

III. Success

13. What does the term "success" for your child mean to you?
14. How would you define "success" in school?
15. Describe the person you hope your child will be when he/she is an adult.
    - What qualities would you like them to have?
    - What are some of the values you would like to pass on to your children?
16. What has been your proudest moment as a parent?
17. Is there anything else you would like to share about your child and family's story?

APPENDIX III: CONSENT AGREEMENT

Children and families in disadvantaged circumstances: Communication, Collaboration and Inclusion

You are being asked to participate in a research study. Before you give your consent to be a volunteer, it is important that you read the following information and ask as many questions as necessary to be sure you understand what you will be asked to do.

Investigators: The principal investigators at the School of Early Childhood Education, Ryerson University are:

Dr. Mehrunnisa Ali, Associate Professor
Dr. Patricia Corson, Associate Professor
Dr. Elaine Frankel, Professor

Description of the Study: The purpose of this project is to increase the ability of providers of public services to respond to families such as yours. Some families may not be as well served either because they are,

- families with children who have developmental disabilities
- families who are newcomers (have been in Canada less than one year)
- families who are socio-economically disadvantaged (receive social assistance, use food banks on a regular basis, live in shelters etc.)

If you and your family agree to participate in this study, a professional family support provider will interview you about your family story. A series of 3-4 interviews with one or more family members present will be held at a location of your choice, at your home or at the family resource centre you attend. Each interview will take about 1 hour. The interview will cover topics about your family's idea of "success" for your pre-school children, the challenges and joys of raising your children and the different agencies and people who help you care for your children. All interviews will be audiotape recorded for later review. You will participate in developing a narrative story of your family with the interviewer at the completion of all interviews. All information that you share during the interview is completely confidential.

You may face some emotional discomfort while talking about difficult times. If you feel uncomfortable, you can ask the researcher to stop the interview at any time, either temporarily or permanently. You will also be given names of trained counsellors you can approach to help you deal with any residual distress.

Benefits of the Study: Although you will not directly benefit from the results of this study, the findings will benefit:

- Individuals and institutions in public health, education, child care and social welfare who work with children and families; as well as individuals receiving in-service and pre-service training for working with children and families
- Policy makers at various levels of government
- Children and families living in disadvantaged circumstances who will ultimately benefit from changes in service providers conceptions of families and hence the supports they offer

Confidentiality: The three Principal Investigators and the family support professional conducting the interview will be the only people with access to the notes and tapes of interviews. All identifying information, such as your names, will be kept confidential. Pseudonyms will be used in any reports or publications. You may request a copy of the summary of your interview within six months of the final interview. The written notes and audiotapes will be kept in a locked office for two years following the completion of the project after which they will be destroyed.

Costs and/or Compensation for Participation: You will be given $250 after the final interview as an honorarium for your family's participation in this study. The honorarium covers time spent and any costs incurred for travelling and child-care.

Voluntary Nature of Participation: Participation in this study is voluntary. Your choice of whether or not to participate will not influence your future relations with Ryerson University. If you decide to participate, you are free to withdraw your consent and to stop your participation at any time without penalty or loss of benefits to which you are allowed.

At any particular point in the study, you may refuse to answer any particular question or stop participation altogether.

Questions about the Study: If you have any questions about the research, please ask. If you have questions later about the research, you may contact.

Dr. Mehrunnisa Ali

416-979-5000 extension 6330

If you have questions regarding your rights as a human subject and participant in this study, you may contact the Ryerson University Research Ethics Board for information.

Research Ethics Board

c/o Office of Research Services

Ryerson University

350 Victoria Street

Toronto, ON M5B 2K3

Agreement:

Your signature below indicates that you have read the information in this agreement and have had a chance to ask any questions you have about the study. Your signature also indicates that you agree to be in the study and have been told that you can change your mind and withdraw your consent to participate at any time. You have been given a copy of this agreement.

You have been told that by signing this consent agreement you are not giving up any of your legal rights.

_____

Name of Participant (please print)

_____   _____

Signature of Participant   Date

_____   _____

Signature of Investigator   Date